"Ace" Any Test

Test

2nd Edition

By
Ron Fry

CAREER PRESS
180 Fifth Avenue
P.O. Box 34
Hawthorne, NJ 07507
1-800-CAREER-1
201-427-0229 (outside U.S.)
FAX: 201-427-2037

Copyright © 1994 by Ron Fry

"ACE" ANY TEST (2ND ED.)

ISBN 1-56414-079-2, $6.95

Cover design by A Good Thing, Inc.

Printed in the U.S.A. by Book-mart Press

To order this title by mail, please include price as noted above, $2.50 handling per order, and $1.00 for each book ordered. Send to: Career Press, Inc., 180 Fifth Ave., P.O. Box 34, Hawthorne, NJ 07507.

Or call toll-free 1-800-CAREER-1 (Canada: 201-427-0229) to order using VISA or MasterCard, or for further information on books from Career Press.

Library of Congress Cataloging-in-Publication Data

Fry, Ronald W.
  "Ace" any test / by Ron Fry. -- 2nd ed.
    p. cm.
  Includes index.
  ISBN 1-56414-079-2
  1. Examinations--United States--Study guides. 2. Test-taking skills--United States. I. Title.
LB3060.57.F79   1994
371.3'02'12--dc20   94-5486
                                                       CIP

CONTENTS

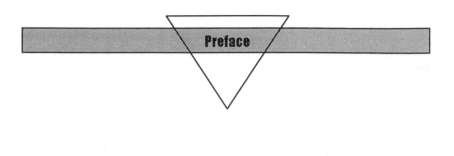

"Ace" Any Test was the last-written (though, interestingly, the first I revised) of the six companion volumes added to the original *How to Study*. All were originally written, or so I thought at the time, for high school students. But over the years I've discovered that the students buying these books are either already in college (which says wonderful things about the preparation they got in high school), in junior high (which says something much more positive about their motivation and, probably, eventual success) or returning to college (about whom more later.)

Many of you reading this are adults. Some of you are returning to school. And some of you are long out of school but have figured out that if you could learn *now* the study skills your teachers never taught you, you'll do better in your careers. All too many of you are parents with the same lament: "How do I get Johnny (Janie) to do better on tests? He (she) knows the material but always gets Cs."

So I want to briefly take the time to address every one of the audiences for this book and discuss some of the factors particular to each of you:

If you're a high school student

You should be particularly comfortable with the format of the book—its relatively short sentences and paragraphs, occasionally humorous (hopefully) headings and subheadings—and the language used. I wrote it with you in mind!

If you're a junior high school student

You are trying to learn how to study at *precisely* the right time. Sixth, seventh and eighth grades—before that sometimes cosmic leap to high school—is without a doubt the period in which all these study skills should be mastered, since doing so will make high school not just easier but a far more positive and successful experience. Although written for high school-level readers, if you're serious enough about studying to be reading this book, I doubt you'll have trouble with the concepts or the language.

If you're a "traditional" college student...

...somewhere in the 18 to 25 age range, I hope you have already mastered reading, note-taking, et al, and are just perusing this book because the GRE is coming.

If you're the parent of a student of any age

You must be convinced of one incontestable fact: It is highly unlikely that your child's school is doing anything to teach him or her how to study. Yes, of course they should. Yes, I know that's what you thought you paid taxes for. Yes, yes, yes. But, but, but—believe me, *they're not doing it.*

How do I know? For one thing, in thousands of interviews on radio, TV and in the print media, my publisher has allowed me to make the same offer: They will give any teacher or school administrator wishing to use any or all of the books in my **HOW TO STUDY** *Program* one *free* book for every one they purchase. That's right, buy 10, get 10 free. Buy 100, get 100 free.

"Ace" Any Test

There are three teachers out there—all three spending *their own money*, mind you—who have taken me up on that offer. Says something about priorities, doesn't it?

I also spend a lot of time talking to students and visiting schools. And the lack of study skills training is woefully obvious, whether the school is in the poorest section of town or the richest, in the inner city or suburban heaven, public or private, elementary, junior high or high school.

They test—oh, how they test! It's gotten to the point where many teachers are spending a lot more time teaching kids what's going to be on some standardized test than the particulars they should be learning, whether or not they will ever show up on a specific test. But many still don't teach any kind of test-taking strategies. When do you guess? What do you answer first, the easiest questions or the hardest? How to you get points on an essay question if you don't have time to write more than a couple of sentences?

Your involvement in your child's education is absolutely essential to his or her eventual success. Surprisingly enough, the results of every study done in the last two decades about what affects a child's success in school concludes that only one factor *overwhelmingly* affects it, every time: parental involvement. Not the size of the school, the number of language labs, how many of the student body go on to college, how many great teachers there are (or lousy ones). All factors, yes. *But none as significant as the effect you can have.*

So please, take the time to read this book (and the others in the series, but especially *How to Study)* yourself. Learn what your kids *should* be learning. (And which of the other five subject-specific books in the Series your child needs the most.)

And you can help tremendously, *even if you were not a great student yourself, even if you never learned great study skills.* You can learn now with your child—not only will it help him or her in school, it will help *you* on the job. Even if you think you need help only in a single area—or two or three—don't use only the specific book in my program that highlights that subject. Read *How to Study* first, *all the way through.* First of all, it will undoubtedly help you increase your mastery of skills you thought you already had. And it will cover those you need help with in a more concise manner. With that background, you will get *more* out of whichever of the other six books you use.

Presuming you need all the help all seven books can give you, what order should you read them in? Aside from reading *How to Study* first—all the way through—I don't think it matters. All of the study skills are interrelated, so practicing one already helps you with the others. If pushed, however, I will admit that I would probably suggest *Improve Your Reading* and *Manage Your Time* be the first two books you study. The former because reading is the basis of every other study skill, the latter because organization is the foundation on which the study pyramid is erected. After that, take your pick!

If you're a nontraditional student

If you're going back to high school, college or graduate school at age 25, 45, 65 or 85—you probably need the help these seven books offer more than anyone! Why? Because the longer you've been out of school, the more likely you don't remember what you've forgotten. And you've forgotten what you're supposed to remember! As much as I emphasize that it's rarely too early to learn good study habits, I must also emphasize that it's never too *late.*

Particular problems of nontraditional students

If you're returning to school and attempting to carry even a partial load of courses while simultaneously holding down a job, raising a family or both, there are some particular problems you face that you probably didn't the first time you were in school:

Time and money pressures. Let's face it, when all you had to worry about was going to school, it simply *had* to be easier than going to school, raising a family and working for a living simultaneously! (And it was!) Mastering all of the techniques of time management is even more essential if you are to effectively juggle responsibilities to your career, family, clubs, friends, etc., with your commitment to school. Money management (which is not covered in this series) may well be another essential skill, whether figuring out how to pay for childcare (something you probably didn't have to worry about the last time you were in high school) or how to manage all your responsibilities while cutting your hours at work to make time for school.

Self-imposed fears of inadequacy. You may well convince yourself that you're just "out of practice" with all this school stuff. You don't even remember what color highlighter to use! While some of this fear is valid, most is not. The valid part is that you are returning to an academic atmosphere, one that you may not have even visited for a decade or two. And it *is* different (which I'll discuss more below) than the "work-a-day" world. That's just a matter of adjustment and, trust me, will take a matter of days, if not hours, to dissipate. But I suspect what many of you are really fearing is that you just aren't in that school "mentality" anymore, that you don't "think" the same way. Or, perhaps more pertinently to this book, that the skills you need to succeed in school are rusty.

I think these last fears are groundless. You've been out there thinking and doing for quite a few years, perhaps very successfully, so it's ridiculous to think school will be so different. It won't be. Relax.

Maybe you're worried because you didn't exactly light up the academic power plant the first time around. Well, neither did

Edison or Einstein or a host of other relatively successful people. But then, you've changed rather significantly since those halcyon days of "boola boolaing," haven't you? Held a series of jobs, raised a family, saved money, taken on more and more responsibility? Concentrate on how much *more* qualified you are for school *now* than you were *then!*

Feeling you're "out of your element"—This is a slightly different fear, the fear that you just don't fit in any more. After all, you are *not* 18 again. But then, neither are fully half the college students on campus today. That's right, fully 50-percent of all college students are older than 25. The reality is, you'll probably feel more in your element now than you did the first time around!

You'll see teachers differently—Probably a plus. It's doubtful you'll have the same awe you did the first time around. At worst, you'll consider teachers your equals. At best, you'll consider them younger and not necessarily as successful or experienced as you are.

There* are *differences in academic life. It's slower than the "real" world, and you may be moving significantly faster than its normal pace. When you were 18, an afternoon without classes meant a game of Frisbee. Now it might mean catching up on a week's worth of errands, cooking (and freezing) a week's worth of dinners and/or writing four reports due last week. Despite your own hectic schedule, do not expect campus life to accelerate in response. You will have to get used to people and systems with far less interest in speed.

I first wrote *How to Study* in 1988, convinced that schools were doing a lousy job of teaching kids to study—synonymous, to me, with teaching them how to *learn*—and that no one was picking up the slack. (I was also convinced—and still am—that most kids wanted *desperately* to learn but would, without some help, find it easier to fail. And failure, once welcomed, is a nasty habit to break.)

Published in 1989, most bookstores wedged one or two copies of *Study* in between the hundreds of phone book-sized test prep volumes. Career Press wasn't a big enough publisher to convince the "chains"—Waldenbooks, Barnes & Noble, B. Dalton—to stock it in any quantity or rich enough to spend any money promoting it.

Need will out. Tens of thousands of people who obviously needed *How to Study* ferreted out copies wherever they lurked and bought them. In 1990, the chains—who *are* smart enough to at least spot a winner the *second* time around—bought 6-copy "pre-packs" and gave the book a little more prominence. (Meaning you didn't have to get a hernia removing other books to find a copy of *Study*.) Career Press sent me around the country to appear on radio and TV, including CNN. And hundreds of newspapers and magazines noticed what we were doing and started writing about *How to Study*. (The fact that test scores had declined for the hundred-fortieth year in a row or so probably had something to do with this, but who am I to quibble with the attention?)

In 1991, *booksellers* started calling to say they hoped I was planning some follow-up books to *Study*. And hundreds of parents and students wrote or called to indicate they needed more help in some specific areas. *Ron Fry's* **HOW TO STUDY** *Program* was born, featuring a second edition of *Study* and four new books— *Improve Your Reading, Manage Your Time, Take Notes and Write Papers*—that delved even deeper into critical study skills. That year I spent more time on the phone doing radio shows than I did, I think, with my wife and 2-year-old daughter.

In 1992, I added two more volumes—*"Ace" Any Test* and *Improve Your Memory*, both of which were pretty much written in response to readers' letters. The latter was, as far as I was concerned, a natural extension of *Improve Your Reading*, which had dealt primarily with the reading process and only peripherally with ways to increase comprehension. *Memory* also delved into problems people faced remembering names, faces, dates, math formulas and a host of others.

Test, on the other hand, was a book I really didn't want to write, since I was (and am) convinced that we are a society tested to death, usually without any clear understanding of what's being tested...or what the results are supposed to mean. Since so many people think learning to study is almost exclusively learning to "take tests," I was also afraid I would undermine my message: Learning how to take a test is a *very* small part of learning how to study. Nevertheless, acknowledging that standardized testing is here to stay meant at least doing my bit to help students do the best they could on the alphabets (SAT, PSAT, ACT, etc., etc., etc.)

Surprisingly, *Test* and *Memory* quickly became the second- and third biggest sellers of the seven books in the series, beaten only by *How to Study*. Evidently, my readers knew darned well what they were requesting.

By the way, in both 1992 and 1993, I added mightily to my Frequent Flyer accounts while talking to people nationwide about studying. I wound up visiting 50 cities, some twice, and appearing on more TV and radio shows than are listed in your daily newspaper.

The result of all this travel was twofold: First, sales of all seven books have skyrocketed, in part because of the chance I've been given to talk about them on so many shows and in so many newspapers and magazines. Second, I got to meet and talk with tens of thousands of students and parents, many of whom confirmed the ongoing need for these books *because very little has changed since I first wrote* **How to Study** *some six years ago.*

"Ace" Any Test

Test scores of every kind are lower today than they were then. More and more students are dropping out or, if they *do* manage to graduate high school, are finding they are not equipped to do *any*thing, whether they're hoping to go to college or trying to land a job. And more and more parents are frustrated by their children's inability to learn and their schools' seeming inability to teach.

With so much new feedback, it was time to revise all seven books, all of which are being published in time for "back to school" in 1994. In every book, I've included additional topics and expanded on others. I've changed some examples, simplified some, eliminated some. I've rewritten sentences, paragraphs or entire sections that students seemed to be struggling with. Most importantly, I've tried to reflect my new understanding of just who is reading these books—"traditional" students, their parents *and* nontraditional (i.e. older, perhaps much older) students, many of those self-same parents—and write in such a way to include all three audiences.

I hope after reading these books you'll agree I've succeeded.

I'm sure after reading these books that *you'll* succeed.

Ron Fry
May, 1994

Chapter One

WHAT ARE YOU AFRAID OF, ANYWAY?

"Life is a test. If you woke up alive this morning, it means you got an 'A' for yesterday."
—Ron Fry

"All we have to fear is fear itself."
—Franklin Delano Roosevelt

FDR was *almost* right. The only thing you *may* have to fear is fear itself. But, frankly, you *don't* have to. You just have to conquer it or beat it into submission so that you can get on with your life—and your history exam.

But it doesn't hurt to have a *little* anxiety. You don't want to become so complacent that you lose that "edge" you need.

Let's spend a few minutes talking about why tests scare people, and then let's help you spend your time studying instead of wasting it on anxiety attacks.

Even famous people do it

I still remember a documentary on a famous singer that I saw on TV years ago. The camera had been following her around while she went to rehearsal, got made-up and talked with her manager.

The scene I remember most was the shot of her as she waited backstage to be announced. Now, remember, this was a woman who had been wowing them for decades. You could hear the audience: It was excited to be in her presence. It was friendly. And she—standing in the wings as the announcer called out her name to loud applause—looked nervous, horrified, petrified, regretful that she'd ever entered show business and extremely vulnerable. (Presuming she remembered she was being filmed, this was the *controlled* panic.)

But, when the announcer called her name and the roar of applause began, she was transformed. She walked with a determined gait to the stage, the lights hit her, she smiled and took the microphone, the band began and she never looked back. Her famous voice filled the auditorium, and the audience went wild. If she could weather such regular panic attacks and still passed the test, why shouldn't you?

A little tension goes a long way

Truly successful entertainers or public speakers will usually admit they get those little knots in their stomachs just before they have to perform. And they would be the first ones to tell you that not only is it OK to go through a nervous moment or two, they actually prefer that—it gives them the adrenaline rush they need to do a good job.

Let's put that back into the context of your exam-taking: You may have taken a test in the past where you thought you knew everything, did little if any studying—and got a bad grade. Don't go too far the other way.

But don't get too tensed up either. Keep a little anxiety in your life. Just keep it under control and in perspective.

Why is there terror present in the first place? Because we don't want to fail. We realize that, within the next 30 or 60 minutes, a percentage of our grade will be determined by what we write or *don't* write down on a piece of paper, or which box we color in with our No. 2 pencil.

So what are you afraid of?

Now, why do some people fail? What does it mean when someone proclaims they don't "test well"? For many, it really means you don't *study* well (or, at the very least, *prepare* well). For others, it could mean they are easily distracted, unprepared for the type of test they are confronting, or simply unprepared mentally to take *any* test (which may well include mentally sabotaging yourself into a poor score or grade, even though you know the material...backwards and forwards.

Take heart—very few people look forward to a test; more of you are afraid of tests than you'd think. But that doesn't mean you *have* to fear them.

Since we all recognize the competitive nature of tests, being in the right frame of mind when taking them is important. Some of us rise to the occasion when facing such a challenge. Others are thrown off balance by the pressure. Both reactions probably have little to do with one's level of knowledge, relative intelligence or amount of preparation. The smartest kids in your class may be the ones most afraid of tests.

Sometimes, it's *not* Fear of Failure—it's Fear of *Success*. "Gee," you think to yourself, "if I do well on this exam, my parents will expect me to do well on the next exam—and the teacher will think I'm going to start doing well every day!"

Fear of success, like martyrdom, is boring. Look at it this way: You'll always have pressure on you throughout your life, so you might as well have *good* pressure ("Hey, genius, keep up the good work!") rather than *bad* pressure ("I can't understand how anyone with a brain like yours makes such bad grades!")

Nobody likes Saralee anyway

One more reason for failure? Some people can't deal with competition. All they can think about is what Saralee is doing. Look at her! She's sitting there, writing down one answer after another—and you just know they're all correct!

Who cares about Saralee? I sure wouldn't. Only one person in that room should be concerned with Saralee and her performance. That's right. Just as only one person should be concerned with *your* performance. Make it all a game: Compete with yourself. See if you can't beat your previous test scores. Now, that's positive competition!

You don't have to join the club

Some people thrive on their own misery and are jealous if you don't thrive on it too. They want to include you in all of their hand-wringing situations, whether you really know (or care) what's happening. These are people to avoid when you're preparing for an exam—the Anxiety Professionals.

"Oh, I'll never learn all this stuff!" they'll cry. You might not win points with Miss Manners if you say, "Well, if you'd shut up and study, you might!" You *can* have the pleasure of thinking it—on your way to a quiet place to study alone.

And watch out for those "friends" who call you the night before the exam with, "I just found out we have to know Chapter 12!" Don't fall into their trap. Instead of dialing 911, calmly remind them that the printed sheet the professor passed out two weeks ago clearly says, "Test on Chapters 6 through 11." Then hang up, get on with your life, and let them wring their hands all the way to the bottom of the grading sheet.

Focus on the exam

If you have trouble concentrating on your preparations for the exam, try this: Think of your life as a series of shoe boxes (the Imelda Marcos Theory). The boxes are all open and lined up in a nice, long, neat row. In each shoe box is a small part of your life—school, work, romantic interests, hobbies, *ad florsheim*. Although you have to move little pieces from one box to another from time to time, you can—and should—keep a lot of this stuff as separate as possible.

Of course, you *can* make it easier to do this by not going out of your way—certainly before an especially big or important test—to add *more* stress to an already stressful life. Two days before the SAT-I is *not* the time to dump a boyfriend, move, change jobs, take out a big loan or create any other waves in your normally placid river of a life.

Is there life after this test?

Yes. And, furthermore, isn't there life *before* this test? Tests are important. They tell the teacher and you how well you're doing in the class (and how well *he or she* is doing in teaching you the material). How many correct answers you get will help you understand how well you know the material.

But, all that aside, a test is only a part of your life. Any one test is not going to ruin your life, it's only going to give you the opportunity to produce a certain grade.

Do your best, using the tips I'm sharing with you in this book, and go forward. And don't, in the process of preparing for an exam, decide that all other forms of life must cease. Maybe you can't devote as much of your time to soaps (but you can tape them for a post-test reward) or even perhaps to those closest to you, but relationships (and soap operas) go on, long after the exams are forgotten.

You're already an expert

You've already taken lots and lots of tests: pop quizzes, oral exams, standardized tests, tests on chapters and units and whole books—and whole semesters. You've done this for years. And, for the most part, you've been successful. And, if you haven't always been as successful as you'd like, keep on reading. For the remainder of this book, we're going to review what you can do to change all that. All this experience, coupled with the real-life "tests" I've already mentioned, demonstrate that you're pretty good—even excellent. Stop a moment and pat yourself on the back. You're a successful test-taker, in spite of a little fright here and there.

One in a million

Just admitting that you're not at ground zero can help you realize that preparing for an exam is not in itself a whole new Task of Life—it's merely part of a continuum.

Think of this fraction: 1 over 1 million. Your life is the big number. This next test is the little number. All the "ones" in your life add up to the 1 million, thus they are important, but, all by themselves, they can't compare to the Giant Economy Number of Life. Write "1/1,000,000" at the top of your next test to remind yourself of that. That alone should kill off a bunch of stomach butterflies.

"Extra" tests give extra help

Here's another tried-and-true suggestion: If you want to practice the many recommendations you're going to get in this book, including what I'm sharing with you in this important first chapter, take a few "extra" tests just to give yourself some practice. It will also help you with overcoming the unacceptable levels of test anxiety.

Get permission from your teachers to retake some old tests to practice the test-taking techniques and exorcising, once and for all, the High Anxiety Demon. And take a couple of standardized tests that your counseling office might have, too, since the color-in-the-box answer sheets and serious questions in printed form have their own set of rules (which, as you can guess, we'll talk about later in this book).

A little perspective, please

The more pressure you put on yourself—the larger you allow a test (and, of course, your hoped-for good scores) to loom in your own mind—the less you are helping yourself. And, of course, the bigger the test really *is,* the more likely you are to keep reminding yourself of its importance.

No matter how important a test really may be to your career—and your scores on some *can* have a major effect on where you go to college, whether you go on to graduate school, whether you get the job you want—it is just as important to *de-emphasize* that test's importance in your mind. This should have no effect on your preparation—you should still study as if your life depended on a superior score. It might!

Keeping the whole experience in perspective might also help: Twenty years from now, nobody will remember, or care, what you scored on *any* test—no matter how life-threatening or life-determining you feel that test is right now.

And don't underestimate that old standby, positive thinking: Thoughts *can* become self-fulfilling prophecies. Tell yourself often enough "be careful, you'll fall over that step," and you probably will. Tell yourself often enough "I'm going to fail this test" and you just might. Likewise, keep convincing yourself that you are as prepared as anyone and are going to "ace" the sucker, and you are already ahead of the game.

Anxiety quotient

To come to terms with the "importance" of a test, read the list below. Knowing the answers to as many of these questions as possible will help reduce your anxiety:

1. What material will the exam cover?
2. How many total points are possible?
3. What percentage of my semester grade is based on this exam?
4. How much time will we have to take the exam?
5. Where will the exam be held?
6. What kinds of questions will be on the exam (matching, multiple-choice, essay, true/false....)?
7. How many points will be assigned to each question? Will essay questions count for 25 percent of the exam

or 50 percent? Will there be five multiple-choice questions or 105?

8. Will it be an open book exam?
9. What can I take in with me? Calculator? Candy bar? Other material crucial to my success?
10. Will I be penalized for wrong answers?

I'm walkin', yes, indeed

Finally, to shake off pre-test anxiety, take a walk. Or a vigorous swim. In the days before an exam, no matter how "big" it is, don't study too hard or all the time or you'll walk into the exam with a fried brain.

And don't think that advice loses its power at the classroom door. Scheduling breaks during tests has the same effect. During a one-hour test, you may not have time to go out for a stroll. But during a two- or three-hour final, there's no reason you should not schedule one, two or even more breaks on a periodic basis—whenever you feel you need them most. Such time-outs can consist of a bathroom stop, a quick walk up and down the hall, or just a minute of relaxation in your seat before you continue the test.

No matter what the time limits or pressures, don't feel you cannot afford such a brief respite. You may need it *most* when you're convinced you can *least* afford it, just as those who most need time management techniques "just don't have the time" to learn them.

Relax, darn it!

If your mind is a jumble of facts and figures, names and dates, you may find it difficult to zero in on the specific details you need to recall, even if you know all the material backwards and forwards. The adrenaline rushing through your system may just make "instant retrieval" impossible.

The simplest relaxation technique is deep breathing. Just lean back in your chair, relax your muscles and take three very deep breaths (count to 10 while you hold each one). For many of you, that's the only relaxing technique you'll ever need.

There are a variety of meditation techniques that may also work for you. Each is based on a similar principle—focusing your mind on one thing to the exclusion of everything else. While you're concentrating on the object of your meditation (even if the object is nothing, a nonsense word or a spot on the wall), your mind can't be thinking about anything else, which allows it to slow down a bit.

Whatever such technique you feel you need to use, re- member an important fact: The more you believe in the tech- nique, the more it will work. Just like your belief that you're going to "ace" that test!

Chapter Two

FINDING THE TIME TO STUDY

"Work expands so as to fill the time available for its completion."
—Cyril Parkinson, Parkinson's Law

"I recommend that you learn to take care of the minutes, for the hours will take care of themselves."
—Lord Chesterfield

Poor time. It really gets a bum rap. We all have problems with it.

We can't slow it down or speed it up.

We can't save it up—all we can do is decide how we're going to spend it.

We invariably need more of it....and don't know where to find it.

Then we wonder where the heck it all went.

But *time* is not really the problem. After all, we all get 24 hours, same for you, me and Saralee. The problem is that most of us have *never been taught how to* manage *our time*...or why we should try. Our parents never sat us down to give us a little "facts of time" talk. And time management skills aren't part of any standard academic curriculum.

In this chapter, let's look at how we can organize our lives so that we have enough time for everything: School, family and friends, work and study.

Let's start by making a major adjustment in our thinking: Time is our friend, not our enemy. Time allows us space in each day or week or month to do the things we enjoy and to reach certain milestones to advance our career, get diplomas or degrees, establish and develop relationships, go on vacations and all that.

And it allows us to prepare for tests. (Let's not get carried away and forget the focus of this book.) This chapter includes some simple time charts that will help you work on *when* and *where* and *how* you manage the various demands on your time.

And, for a whole book on the subject, don't forget that I've already written, and recently updated, *Manage Your Time*, one of the six other books in my **HOW TO STUDY** *Program*. *Manage Your Time* outlines ways that will help you in even more detail, and covers even more aspects of your life as a student.

The management of time

"Time management" has become a big business in America. You can find a course on this topic in the catalog of any community college or adult-education program in the country. Some corporations send their entire work force to take time managment seminars.

Stick with me. Instead of paying hundreds of dollars for such a course, pay close attention to what's in this chapter.

Look at it this way: Between now and next Tuesday, whether you are preparing to play in the state basketball tournament, writing a paper on the Mississippi Delta or holding down three jobs (or, heaven help you, all of the above), you have exactly the same amount of time as the rest of us. It's what you *do* with that time that makes the difference.

How are you going to get from here to then? Are you just going to go crashing along, like an elephant trampling down banana trees? Or are you going to get there with a plan? Good. That's the right answer. (See? You just passed *another* test. Congratulations.)

You're spending three hours a day *resting?*

The first step to overhaul your current routine is to *identify* that routine, in detail. My suggestion is to chart, in 15-minute increments, how you spend every minute of every day *right now.* While a day or two might be sufficient for some of you, I recommend you chart your activities for an entire week, including the weekend.

This is especially important if, like many people, you have huge pockets of time that seemingly disappear, but, in reality, are devoted to things like "resting" after you wake up, putting on make-up or shaving, reading the paper, waiting for transportation or driving to and from school or work, etc. Could you use an extra hour or two a day, either for studying or for fun? Make better use of such "dead" time and you may well find all the time you need.

For example, learn how to do multiple tasks at the same time. Listen to a book on tape while you're working around the house; practice vocabulary or math drills while you're driving; have your kids, parents or roommates quiz you for an upcoming test while you're doing dishes, vacuuming or dusting; *always* carry your calendar, notebook(s), pens, and a textbook with you—you can get a phenomenal amount of reading or studying done while on line at the bank, in the library, at the supermarket or on a bus or train.

The more ready you are to transform "dead" time into study time, the more ways you'll invent to do so.

The vital statistics

How often have you made a "to-do" list and then either forgotten it, lost it or ignored it? To-do lists have incredible merits if you do them right. But they're not much good if you don't use them.

Let's run through the composition and execution of a to-do list for a shopping expedition as an example. Here's what I do when I am making up a list of run-around-town errands:

First, after writing down where I have to go, I turn the paper over and make individual lists of items for each stopping place. I may have Smith's Drugstore on the "where to go" front side of the list, but on the back I have listed shaving cream, bubble gum, newspaper, hair spray, prescription.

Am I (A) compulsive-obsessive or (B) merely organized?

If this were a real test, the right answer would be (B).

By separating the *where* from the *what*, I am able to focus on getting from the post office to the drugstore to the hardware store without trying to separate the toothpaste from the tool kit. On the other hand, when I am heading down Aisle 3B, I can concentrate on what items I need from this particular stop.

I number the *where* side (putting a "1" beside my first stop, a "2" by the second and so on) so that I can do a "no brainer"— I have quickly figured out in what order I need or want to do the shopping, and I don't have to stop to think where to go next. I just consult the list.

I devised this simple addition to my list-making because I had spent too many Saturday mornings driving back and forth in an almost random fashion or sitting in a parking lot saying to myself, "Now, where should I go next? The drugstore? No, that's near the video store. That means I should..."

Take a whole five minutes at home and write down the 1, 2, 3, etc., and then go for it.

I do one more thing on my shopping list: If I need to take anything with me (return a video, drop off cleaning, photocopy an article, etc.), I place a "T" with a circle around it beside the place I need the "T" item for. That way, I don't get to Smith's only to discover that I forgot to bring the prescription form. (If convenient, put all the "T" items, along with the list, beside the door so you won't have to go searching for them when it's time to leave.)

Now, why am I sharing all this detailed information on my shopping-list habits when we're supposed to be talking about getting ready for your zoology exam? Because the methods and the rationale are similar to your management of time. Here's what my list does for me:

- I don't forget anything.
- I save time.
- It's quick and easy.
- I "save" my brain for what's important.

Attention, Study-Mart shoppers!

Think of the time between now and your next exam as your shopping trip. You want to use this time most effectively so that you: (1) don't forget anything; (2) work efficiently (save time); (3) arrange your studying so that it's done as quickly and as easily as possible; and (4) concentrate on the important details, not on *all* the details (big difference!).

How much time do you have? Unless I missed something in the paper this morning, we all have 24 hours a day. But you and I know that's not what we're talking about here. We have to subtract sleeping, eating, commuting and obligations like work and classes...whoa! Any time left?

Sure there is. But, first, you need to get a handle on what you *must* do, what you *should* do and what you *want* to do. Let's refer to them as our H, M and L priorities.

The H ("High") priorities are those things we *must* do between now and the next test.

The M ("Medium") priorities are those things we *should* do, but could postpone without being jailed or written out of the will.

The L ("Low") priorities are those things we live for but are *expendable*. At least, they're expendable until you've finished taking this next exam. (*Time-saving Tip:* If you push aside the same low-priority item day after day, week after week, at some point you should just stop and decide whether it's something you need to do at all! This is a strategic way to make a task/problem "disappear.")

Yes, Virginia, it's all right to sleep

An "H" priority is sleeping and eating and attending class, especially the class in question. (You simply can't ignore these.)

An "M" is getting your family car's oil changed or taking your cat to the vet for a checkup. (Important, but unless the car's dipstick shows that it has no oil or the cat is so sick it's trying to dial the vet itself, these tasks can be delayed for a handful of days.)

An "L" is going to the Hitchcock Film Festival or partying with friends up at the cabin in the mountains.

In *Manage Your Time*, I gave you three different forms to use. I'm including them in this book as well. The first one, the Term Planning Calendar, helps you sort out and manage the big picture. The second, Priority Tasks This Week, breaks the semester down to seven-day periods. And the third, Daily Schedule, will reduce it to a focused day-by-day format. (Note: A fourth tool—the Project Board—is not easily transformed to the size of this book but is, nevertheless, a very important element in any time-management system. See the new second edition of *Manage Your Time* for a detailed discussed of the Project Board and how to use it.) ´

These charts are intended to cover all aspects of your life from social events to final exams. Let's look again at these forms in light of preparing for and taking tests.

An endearing term

Let's talk about the Term Planning Calendar, on page 41, first. Simply put, this is a series of monthly calendars with all the important events listed on them. Sounds pretty simple. Actually, it is. Even if you've only got six weeks left in the semester, go ahead and fill out one of these.

Don't just list the school-related items ("Biology Semester Exam, 9 a.m." on May 3); put down the "H" items from the rest of your life, too ("Trip to Chicago" on March 22).

One very good reason for listing all the social/personal/non-academic items is for you to determine which of those are going to remain in the "H" category. For example, if you discover that you have planned a trip to Chicago for the weekend before your French mid-term the following Monday, you'd better cry *"Sacre bleu!"* and decide the Chicago trip is an "L" and must be moved to another time.

Get the picture?

One of the most important reasons for writing down what exactly is coming up is to get that Big Picture. Once you've filled in all the due dates of term papers, unit tests, mid-terms, finals, project reports, etc., take a good look at the results.

Are there a bunch of deadlines in the same week or even on the same day? During finals and mid-terms, of course, this really can't be helped and there's no way to take the tests at another time.

But perhaps you can do something about some of the other deadlines. If you have a French test covering three units on the same day that you have to turn in a paper on the "Influence of the Beatles on British Foreign Policy" and a status report on your gerbil project for sociology, take the plunge and decide that you will get the paper and the project status report done early so that you can devote the time just prior to that day to studying for your French test.

You can't make decisions like that, however, if you can't sit back and get an overall view. (I like to sit back literally and look at the Term Planning Calendar so I can easily see where several deadlines are on the same day or week.)

Looking at everything that is coming up will help you decide what is really an "H" and what is not. It need not cut into your social life, but it does mean that you may need to rearrange some things or say "no" to some invitations that fall smack in the middle of gerbil data-gathering time.

But you can have fun and frolic on the nights and weekends that are far enough away from your "H" priorities. And, when personal "H" events come up (you really can't miss your sister's wedding no matter how much the gerbils need you), your Term Planning Calendar gives you enough warning so that you can make sure your school work doesn't suffer.

"I should have planned better"

Once you have a grasp of your obligations for a term at a time, bring the tasks down to the week at hand by filling out the Priority Tasks This Week form (see the sample on page 42). When planning study time for a test during the week, find the answers to these two questions: (1) "How much time do I *need* to devote to studying for this exam?" and (2) "How much time do I *have* to study for this exam?"

It's fairly easy to determine the answer to the second question. After all, there are a finite number of hours between now and the exam and you are filling in the "H" priorities and figuring that a certain amount of time devoted to sleeping and eating is necessary.

But the first question calls for a fairly definitive answer, too, or else you will never be able to plan.

Consider these other questions when figuring the time needed:

- How much time do I usually spend studying for this type of exam? What have been the results? (If you usually spend three hours and you consistently get Ds, perhaps you need to reassess the time you're spending or, more accurately, *mis*spending .)
- What grade do I have going for me now? (If it's a solid B and you're convinced you can't get an A and you are content with a B, you may decide to devote less time to studying for the exam than if you have a C+ and an extra-good grade on the exam will give you a solid B. Just make sure you aren't overconfident and end up with an exam grade that will ruin your B forever.)
- What special studying do I have to do? (It's one thing to review notes and practice with a study group—more on that later in the book—but if you need to sit in a language lab and listen to hours of tapes or run the

slower group of gerbils through the alphabet once more, plan your time accordingly.)

- Organize the materials you need to study, pace yourself and check to see how much material you have covered in the first hour of review. How does this compare to what you have left to study? Not every hour will be of equal merit (some hours, for whatever reason, will be more productive than others, while some material will take you longer to review), but you should be able to gauge pretty well from this first hour and from your previous experience.

Be careful how you "divvy up" your study time. Schedule enough time for the task, but not so much time that you "burn out." Every individual is different, but most students study best for blocks of about one and a half to three hours, depending on the subject. You might find history fascinating and be able to read for hours. Calculus, on the other hand, may be a subject that you can best handle in "small bites," a half-hour to an hour at a time.

Don't overdo it. Plan your study time in blocks, breaking up work time with short leisure activities. It's helpful to add these to your schedule as well. You'll find that these breaks help you think more clearly and creatively when you get back to studying.

Even if you tend to like longer blocks of study time, be careful about scheduling study "marathons"—a six- or eight-hour stretch rather than a series of two-hour sessions. The longer the period you schedule, the more likely you'll have to fight the demons of procrastination. Convincing yourself that you are really studying your heart out, you'll also find it easier to justify time-wasting distractions, scheduling longer breaks, and, before long, quitting before you should.

Don't be dazed

Now we get to the Daily Schedule (see the sample on page 43), the piece of paper that will keep you sane as you move through the day.

Your Term Planning Calendar will most likely be on the wall beside your study area in your dorm, apartment or house. Your Priority Tasks This Week should be carried with you so that you can add any items that come up in class ("Oh," your teacher says, "did I forget to tell you that we have a quiz on Friday on the first two chapters?") or in conversation ("Go skiing with you this weekend? With you *and* your gorgeous twin? Let me check my calendar!").

Carry your Daily Schedule so that you can be sure not to forget *anything*. The Daily Schedule is divided into four categories:

1. **Assignments Due.** What has to be turned in on this day. Check before you leave for class. (This is like the "T" notations on my shopping list.)

2. **To Do/Errands.** Don't depend on your memory. It's not that you can't remember; it's that you don't *need* to remember. This column will help you plan ahead (e.g., actually buying a birthday present *before* the birthday) and save you last-minute panics when you should be studying for the upcoming exam.

   As with any to-do list, make sure each item is really an item and not a combination of several steps (or stops). "Phone home" is one item; "arrange details for spring dance" is not.

3. **Homework.** When the teacher gives out homework assignments, here's where you can write them down so they're all together, complete with due dates, page numbers and any other information from the teacher.

4. Schedule. The actual list of events for the day from early morning to late at night. This is especially important when you have something extraordinary happening. For example, suppose that your teacher tells you to meet her in a different room for your 9:30 biology class. Again, if you depend on your memory alone, you will most likely be the only one who isn't getting to dissect a frog over in McGillicuddy Hall.

In fact, you should highlight any unusual happenings like that with a brightly colored pen just to remind yourself. And take a moment to glance over the day's schedule *twice*: Look at it the night before, to psych yourself up for the coming day and make sure you didn't forget to do any special assignments. Then, glance at it again while you are having a quiet moment during your nutritious breakfast.

Using these time-saving tools effectively

Organizing your life requires you to actually *use* these tools. Once you have discovered habits and patterns of study that work for you, continue to use and hone them.

Plan according to *your* schedule, *your* goals and *your* aptitudes, not some ephemeral "standard." Allocate the time you expect a project to take *you*, not the time it might take someone else, how long your teacher says it should take, etc.

Try to be realistic and honest with yourself when determining those things that require more effort, those that come easier to you.

Whenever possible, schedule pleasurable activities *after* study time, not before. They will then act as incentives, not distractions.

Be flexible and be ready. Changes happen and you'll have to adjust your schedule to accommodate them.

Monitor your progress at reasonable periods and make changes where necessary. Remember, this is *your* study regimen—you conceived it, you can change it.

If you find that you are consistently allotting more time than necessary to a specific chore—giving yourself one hour to review your English notes every Sunday but always finishing in 45 minutes or less—change your future schedule accordingly. You may use the extra 15 minutes for a task that consistently takes *longer* than you've anticipated or, if such doesn't exist, quit 15 minutes early. Isn't scheduling great?

As assignments are entered on your calendar, make sure you also enter items needed—texts, other books you have to buy, borrow or get from the library, special materials (drawing pad, magic markers, graph paper, etc.).

You may decide that color coding your calendar—red for assignments that must be accomplished that week, blue for steps in longer-term assignments, yellow for personal time and appointments, green for classes, etc.—makes it easier for you to tell at a glance what you need to do and when you need to do it.

Once you're used to your class schedule, you may decide to eliminate classes from your calendar and make it less complicated.

Adapt these tools to your own use. Try anything you think may work—use it if does, discard it if it doesn't.

Do your least favorite chores (study assignments, projects, whatever) first—you'll feel better having gotten them out of the way! And plan how to accomplish them as meticulously as possible. That will get rid of them even faster.

If you see that you are moving along faster than you anticipated on one task or project sequence, there is absolutely nothing wrong with continuing onto the next part of that assignment or the next project step.

If you are behind, don't panic. Just take the time to reorganize your schedule and find the time you need to make up. You may be able to free up time from another task, put one part of a long-term project off for a day or two, etc.

The tools we've discussed and the various other hints, etc. should get you into the habit of writing things down. Not having to remember all these items will free up space in your brain for the things you need to concentrate on or *do* have to remember.

Some things you do can be picked up or dropped at any time. Beware of those time-consuming and complicated tasks that, once begun, demand to be completed. Interrupting at any point might mean starting all over again. What a waste of time *that* would be!

If you're writing and have a brainstorm—just as the phone rings (and you know it's from that person you've been waiting to hear from all week)—take a minute to at least jot down your ideas before you stop.

Nothing can be as counterproductive as losing your concentration, especially at critical times. Learn to ward off those enemies that would alter your course and you will find your journey much smoother.

One way to guard against these mental intrusions is to know your own study clock and plan your study time accordingly. Each of us is predisposed to function most efficiently at specific times of the day (or night). Find out what sort of study clock you are on and schedule your work during this period.

Beware of uninvited guests and *all* phone calls: Unless you are ready to take a break, they will only get you off schedule.

More subtle enemies include the sudden desire to sharpen every pencil in the house, an unheard-of urge to clean your room, an offer to do your sister's homework. Anything, in other words, to avoid your own work. If you find yourself doing anything *but* your work, either take a break then and there or pull yourself together and get down to work. Self-discipline, too, is a learned habit that gets easier with practice.

The simple act of saying "no!" (to others or to yourself) will help insulate yourself from these unnecessary (and postponable) interruptions. Remember, what you are seeking to achieve is not just time—but *quality* time. Put your "do not disturb" sign up and stick to your guns, no matter what the temptation.

In line with my advice above, there *are* times to ignore the schedule, pat yourself on the back and take off and lie on the grass. Incorporate "reward time" into your regular schedule? This could mean a night off every week to do something you like, a weekend a month, etc. Alternatively, each day (if you really need help, each *hour*) you could simply set up a reward as an incentive for finishing an assignment, a project, a day's work, whatever.

Going into "test-training"

Now that you have discovered the value of keeping track of upcoming events, including exams—and the possibility that you can actually plan ahead and keep your life from getting too crazy even during finals week—we can talk a little about the days prior to the exams themselves.

If you have an upcoming exam early in the morning and you are afraid you won't be in shape for it, do a bit of subterfuge on your body and brain.

Get up early for several days before the exam, have a good breakfast, and do homework or review your notes. This will help jump-start your body and brain and get used to the idea of having to solve equations or think seriously about the Punjab at an earlier-than-usual hour.

On the other end of the day, take care to get to bed early enough. Forego the late-night parties and the midnight movie on TV and actually devote enough time to getting some serious ZZZZZs.

Cramming *doesn't* work

In case I didn't mention it yet, **cramming does not work.** We've all done it at one time or another, with one excuse or another—waited until the last minute and then tried to cram a week's or month's or entire semester's worth of work into a single night or weekend. Did it work for you? I doubt it.

After a night of no sleep and too much coffee, most of us are lucky if we remember where the test *is* the next morning. A couple of hours later, trying to stay awake long enough to make it back to bed, we not only haven't learned anything, we haven't even done very well on the test we crammed for!

How to cram anyway

Nevertheless, despite your resolve, best intentions and firm conviction that cramming is a losing proposition, you may well find yourself—though hopefully not too often—in the position of needing to do *some*thing the night before a test you haven't studied for at all. If so, there are some rules to follow that will make your night of cramming at least marginally successful:

Be realistic about what you can do. You absolutely *cannot* master a semester's worth of work in a single night. The *more* information you try to cram in, the *less* effective you will be.

Be selective and study in depth. The more you've managed to miss, the more selective you need to be in organizing your cram session. You *can't* study it all. It really is better in this case to know a lot about a little rather than a little about a lot.

Massage your memory. Use every memory technique you know (and the additional ones in **Improve Your Memory**) to maximize what you're able to retain in your short-term memory.

Know when to give up. When you can't remember your name, give up and get some sleep. Better to arrive at the exam with some sleep under your belt and feeling as relaxed as possible.

Consider an early morning rather than a late-night cram. Especially if you're a "morning" person but even if you're not, I've personally found it more effective to go to bed early and get up early rather than go to bed late and get up exhausted.

Spend the first few minutes writing down whatever you remember now but are afraid you will forget. A suggestion good at any time but especially when your mind is trying to hold onto so many facts and figures it seems ready to explode.

As time goes by

Be honest with yourself. Don't block out two hours of study for your calculus exam *today* when you suspect your best friend will entice you to go with him to get a pizza and talk about anything *but* calculus. If you have budgeted six hours total to prepare for the exam, you've just cheated yourself out of a whole third of the time.

It's OK, in fact, to write down "pizza with Dave" for those two hours. Just be realistic and honest and budget your true study time when you will truly be studying.

Studying with kids

So many more of you are going back to school while raising a family, I want to add some particular tidbits of advice for studying while screaming rug rats are gnawing at your legs:

Plan activities to keep the kids occupied. And out of your hair. The busier you are in school and/or at work, the more time your kids will want you when you *are* home. If you spend a little time with them, it may be easier for them to play alone, especially if you've planned ahead, creating projects *they* can work on while *you're* working on your homework.

Make the kids part of your study routine. Kids love routine, so include them in yours. If 5:30 to 7:30 is always "Dad's Study Time," they will soon get used to it, especially if you make spending other time with them a priority and take the time to give them something to do during those hours. Explaining the importance of what you're doing—in a way that includes some ultimate benefit for *them*—will also motivate them to be part of your "study team."

Use the television as a baby-sitter. While many of you will have a problem with this, it may be the lesser of two evils.

Plan your study accordingly. All of these things will probably *not* keep your kids from interrupting every now and then. So don't try to eliminate them—plan your schedule *to incorporate them.* Take more frequent breaks to spend five minutes with your kids— they'll be more likely to give you the fifteen or twenty minutes at a time *you* need if they get periodic attention themselves. By default, *that* means avoiding projects that can only be done with an hour of massive concentration—you can only work in fifteen or twenty minute bursts!

Find help. Spouses can occasionally take the kids out for dinner and a movie, relatives can baby-sit (at their homes) on a rotating basis, playmates can be invited over (allowing you to send your darling to their house the next day), you may be able to trade baby-sitting chores with other parents at school, and professional daycare may be available at your child's school or in someone's home for a couple of hours a day. Be creative in finding the help you need and scheduling accordingly.

Term Planning Calendar

Fill In due dates for assignments and papers, dates of tests, and important non-academic activities and events

Month	Mon	Tue	Wed	Thu	Fri	Sat	Sun

"Ace" Any Test

Priority Rating	Scheduled?	Priority Tasks This Week Week of ▢▢▢ through ▢▢▢

Daily Schedule   *date:* ____

Assignments Due

| |
| |
| |
| |
| |

To Do/Errands

| |
| |
| |
| |
| |
| |
| |
| |

Homework

| |
| |
| |
| |
| |

Schedule

5	
6	
7	
8	
9	
10	
11	
12	
1	
2	
3	
4	
5	
6	
7	
8	
9	
10	
11	
12	

Chapter Three

WHEN SHOULD YOU REALLY START STUDYING FOR THAT TEST?

"He listens well who takes notes."
— Dante (1265-1321)

Once upon a time, there was a hard-working student named Melvin. He read his textbooks, took good notes in class, rarely missed a day of school, and always did his homework. Sitting next to him in class was a guy named Steve. This guy *sort of* took notes, *kind of* read his textbook, and *usually* did his homework. Well, OK, not usually but *kind of* usually—if he came to class at all.

The day of the big test came. Hard-working Melvin got a D and slouchy, lazy Steve got an A.

If you believe this bears any resemblance to reality, please read and reread every one of the seven books in my **HOW TO STUDY *Program***. You need all the help you can get.

The first day of the test of your life

Well, maybe I shouldn't really say "test of your life." It sounds as if you may not come out of this one alive. Even the new SAT-I isn't that important or scary!

What I really want to emphasize in this chapter was hinted at in the "once upon a time" story above: You don't start preparing for a test a couple of days before. You begin when you walk into the classroom on the first day—or even *before* that.

Everything you do in that course—attending every class, applying listening skills, taking good notes, doing your homework and reading all the assignments—helps you in "studying" for the exam.

Too many students think the exam is out there all by itself—floating out in space like a balloon that got loose from a bawling kid at a carnival. Nope. The role of the exam would be better described as a slice of pie with other "slices"—note taking, attendance, homework, etc.

For whom the alarm clock tolls

Yes, my friend, it may be cruel and it may be cold, but getting out of bed and going to class is the first step toward passing the final that's four months away.

"Oooh, missing that biology class just this one time can't huuuuurrrrrrt!" you moan as you roll over and bury your head under the pillow. "Why, oh why did I stay up so late?" you whine. "Why, oh why," you cry, "did I forget to iron something to wear?" "Why, oh why," you add, "was I ever born!"

Obviously, if this is you, you've got to start by getting to bed a little bit earlier, planning ahead a little bit more, and deciding that going to class is something you must do automatically.

Now that you're here...

All right. I've got you out of bed (and into a reasonably ironed outfit, I presume) and inside the classroom. You're awake, polite, respectful and listening. Now what?

Actually, that question needed to have been asked last night or several nights ago. You can't just waltz into class and be up to speed. When you arrive, you're expected by your teacher to have already accomplished the following:

1. You have read the assignment.
2. You have brought your notes/textbooks with you.
3. You have brought your homework assignment.
4. You have opened your notebook to the right page, opened the textbook to the current chapter and got out your homework to hand it in—all by the time the bell rings.

Is all of that cruel and inhuman punishment? Am I trying to make you into a student from a wildly competitive society somewhere along the Pacific Rim? No, I'm merely giving you a list of what will help you get the most out of the class—*long* before the test day arrives.

Pop goes the quiz

Not all tests, as you surely know by now, are announced. Your friendly neighborhood teacher may decide, out of malice, boredom or his lesson-plan book, to give you a pop quiz.

Now, how can you score well if you, first of all, aren't even in class and, second of all, haven't read the new material and periodically reviewed the old? And suppose it's an open book test and you don't have a book to open?

Let's face it. Biology or U.S. history or economics or whatever 101 may not be your favorite subject but that doesn't mean you have to have an attitude about it. "Proving" you can't or won't do well in a class proves nothing.

Before that bell rings for class to begin, do all those things I listed above. Have your work ready to go so you don't waste time trying to find everything. Of course, if you've done a last-minute check back home or in the dorm, you'll know for sure that you've got the right books, notebooks, homework assignments, etc. Teachers get really tired of hearing, "I left it at home/in the car/in the dorm/with my girlfriend."

The next steps

Let's move on to what you should do during class, after class and before class.

First, during class, as we've already said, you need to listen. Not a difficult task, even when the teacher isn't going to win any elocution awards.

Teachers like to see students take notes. It shows them that you are interested in the topic at hand and that you think enough of what is being said to write it down. (And, if you've ever stood at the front of the room, you can usually tell who's taking notes and who's writing a letter to that friend in Iowa.)

Another of the books in this **HOW TO STUDY** *Program* is called *Take Notes*. As you can imagine, it goes into much more detail than I will here on taking good class notes. Let me deal, here, with *how* and *why* notes will help you study for—and pass—an exam.

First, a great deal of the material on most exams will come from your notes. A very good reason for never missing class. Even if you have to miss class (other students and the teacher would prefer that you remain home if you have a contagious tropical fever), you can get someone else's notes. On an occasional basis, this is OK. But you don't want to do this too often.

They are, after all, your friend's notes, not yours. Your friend has slightly different study habits, a slightly different body of knowledge to bring to class and different methods of concentration. He will not always write down things you would have because he knows them already or he was looking out the window at two squirrels playing touch football with a walnut. On the other hand, he will fill up half his pages with stuff that you would have skipped entirely because you know it's right there on page 99 of your textbook (which you read and he didn't).

You are your own best note-taker

I'm sure you've observed in your classes that some people are constantly taking notes. Others end up with two lines on one page. Most of us fall somewhere in between.

The person who never stops taking notes is either writing a letter to that friend in Iowa or has absolutely no idea what *is* or is *not* important.

The results are dozens of pages of notes (by the end of the semester) that may or may not be helpful. This person is so busy writing down stuff that he isn't prepared or even aware that he can ask and answer questions to help him understand the material better. To use that old adage, he can't see the forest for the trees. He is probably the same person who takes a marking pen and underlines or highlights every word in the book.

Contrast him to the person who thinks note-taking isn't cool, so he only writes down today's date and the homework assignment. He may write something when the teacher says, "Now, write this down and remember it," but he probably just scribbles some nonsense words. After all, he's cool.

Watch him sweat when it's time to study for the exam. He's stuck with a faulty memory and a textbook that may not contain half the material that will be on the test.

Notes: Tools of the trade

For a time, I found it very useful to type my notes after I'd written them in class. First of all, my handwriting won't win any prizes. (I noticed early on that very few people asked to borrow my notes. "Is this word 'Madagascar' or 'Muncie'?" they'd ask a little too loudly.)

Second, typing the notes gave me an opportunity to have a quick review of the class, spell out most of my abbreviations and—most importantly—discover if I missed anything. This gave me time to check my textbook or ask a classmate for the missing information. You don't want to discover this at midnight the night before the test.

A neater version of my notes was also extremely helpful when it came time to study for the test. I could read what was there, I had highlighted the most important elements, and the whole batch of notes just made more sense.

Why did I say I did this "for a time"? Because I stopped doing it my second year of college and haven't done it since. I concluded that the "cons"—primarily the time I was wasting— just outweighed the "pros" discussed above. Instead, 1 concentrated on developing my own shorthand system that minimized the need to rewrite anything and maximized my ability to capture "note-worthy" material the first (and only) time around.

Looks aren't everything, but...

You'll want *your* class notes to be as readable and "study-able" as possible.

"Ace" Any Test

You don't have to be a master of shorthand to streamline your note-taking. Here are five ways:

1. *Eliminate vowels.* As a sign that was ubiquitous in the New York City subways used to proclaim, "If u cn rd ths, u cn gt a gd jb." (If you can read this, you can get a good job.)
2. *Use word beginnings* ("rep" for representative, "con" for congressperson) and other easy-to-remember abbreviations.
3. *Stop putting periods* after all abbreviations (they add up!)
4. *Use standard symbols* in place of words. Here is a list that will help you out in most of your classes (you may recognize many of these symbols from math and logic):

≈	*Approximately*
w/	*With*
w/o	*Without*
wh/	*Which*
→	*Resulting in*
←	*As a result of/consequence of*
+	*And or also*
*	*Most importantly*
cf	*Compare; in comparison; in relation to*
ff	*Following*
<	*Less than*
>	*More than*
=	*The same as, equal to*
↑	*Increasing*

↓	*Decreasing*
esp	*Especially*
△	*Change*
⊂	*It follows that*
∴	*Therefore*
∵	*Because*

5. **Create your own symbols** and abbreviations based on your needs and comfort-level.

There are two specific symbols I think you'll want to create—they'll be needed again and again:

Ⓦ That's my symbol for "*What?*", as in "what the heck does that mean", "what did she say?" or "What happened? I'm completely lost!" It denotes *something* that's been missed—leave space in your notes to fill in the missing part of the puzzle after class.

Ⓜ That's my symbol for "My idea" or "My thought." I want to clearly separate my own thoughts during a lecture from the pro-fessor's—put in too many of your own ideas (without noting that they *are* yours) and your notes begin to lose some serious value!

Feel free to use your own code for these two important instances; you certainly don't have to use mine.

While I recommend using all the "common" symbols and abbreviations listed previously *all* the time, in *every* class, in order to maintain consistency, you may want to create specific symbols or abbreviations for each class. In chemistry, for example, "TD" may stand for thermodynamics, "K" for the Kinetic Theory of Gases (but don't mix it up with the "K" for

Kelvin). In history, "GW" is the Father of our country, "ABE" is Mr. Honesty, "FR" could be French Revolution (or "freedom rider"), "IR", industrial revolution.

How do you keep everything straight? No matter what, summarize your abbreviations on each class's notes, perhaps on the front page in a corner. If you're a little more adventurous, create a list on the first page of that class's notebook or binder section for the abbreviations and symbols you intend to use regularly through the semester.

Reading is fundamental

Reading improves reading. In other words, if you hate reading or if you consider yourself a slow reader, keep at it anyway. Read anything and everything. Read at nights and on weekends. Read cereal boxes (even though the ingredients can be as scary as a Stephen King novel) and newspapers and magazines and short stories and....well, you get the idea.

As you may have guessed by now, there's a volume in my **HOW TO STUDY** *Program* on this topic, too. It's called *Improve Your Reading* (available in a brand-new second edition too) and, like the other books I've mentioned, it provides a lot of detail on how you can get more out of your reading.

Let's look at how you can use your reading skills—and improve them—to get higher grades. Here are some suggestions that help people read more efficiently:

1. When a chapter in a textbook has questions at the end, read the questions first. Why? They will give you an idea of what the chapter is all about and they will be "clues" as to what you should look for in the text.

2. Underline or highlight main points in the text. Don't, like our friend I mentioned earlier, mark too much or your efforts will be meaningless. At the same time, pay special attention to words and phrases the author has "highlighted" by placing them in italics or in boldface.

3. Don't skip over the maps, charts, graphs, photos or drawings. Much of this information may not also be in the text. If you skip it, you're skipping vital information.

4. What's the "big picture" here? We can get bogged down in the footnotes and unfamiliar words and lose touch with the purpose of the chapter. Review subheads, margin notes and questions and discussion points to get a grasp of the big picture.

5. Keep a balancing act between class discussions and notes, on the one hand, and the textbook (and any other workbooks) on the other. They will complement each other in their content. Let's suppose that you've read Chapter 8 already ("Japan and China in the 19th Century") and now you've discussed and taken notes on the same topic at least once in class.

   Sit down at your desk with both notes and Chapter 8 in front of you. Add information from the book to your notes but add it in this way: "10 reasons why opium trade flourished, pp. 112-113." Don't write down the 10 reasons since they are right there in the book, all neatly printed for you. But do this kind of cross-referencing so that you integrate the book with the notes.

6. Shortly before class, look over the chapter once again. Review what you and the author have decided

are the most important points and mark topics you want to ask the teacher to explain. (It's much better to have real questions rather than decide you're going to look smart by having a quota of questions each time. Teachers know the difference.)

The best time to study for your next class is right after the last one. Let's say you have Government 101 at 9:30 a.m. on Monday, Wednesday and Friday. As soon as you can after your Monday class, review that day's class notes, fill in anything you missed (including questions to raise later) and complete the reading assignment and other homework that's due on Wednesday.

Why? Because the class is fresh in your mind. Your notes are crying to be reviewed and corrected or added to, and you have a level of understanding that may not be there Tuesday night at 9 p.m.

Then, spend a little time on the same class and the same materials as close as possible to the next class. Let's say you can do that at 8:30 a.m. on Wednesday. The *big* study time is ASAP after Monday's class; the little *quick-let's-review* time comes shortly *before* Wednesday's class.

Now, let's refine these study habits for the next test. Follow me to Chapter 4, please.

Chapter Four

HOW TO STUDY SMARTER, NOT HARDER

"You have to study a great deal to know a little."
—Charles de Secondat, Baron de Montesquieu (1689-1755)

The baron thought he knew what he was talking about. And he did, but he said that in the days before books like the one you're holding were written. I'm going to be so bold as to amend what he said: "You have to study a reasonable amount to know a great deal."

Why change his centuries-old words? Because we know a lot about study techniques that he didn't. We also have the advantage of a lot of modern conveniences (I'm talking about such things as language labs, not MTV). And because we can concentrate on studying *smarter*, not harder.

Enough baron-bashing. Let's look at how we can study "a reasonable amount" and do well on the exams that are intended to find out if we know what we think we do.

Where should you study?

If you've never asked yourself this question—assuming that "home is where the heart" and the books are—take the time to discover both where you're most comfortable and most effective. Here are the possibilities:

At the library. And there may be numerous choices, from the large reading room, to quieter, sometimes deserted specialty rooms, to your own study cubicle.

At home. Just remember that this is the place where distractions are most likely to occur. No one tends to telephone you at the library and little brothers (or your own kids) will not tend to find you easily in the "stacks."

At a friend's, neighbor's or relative's. This may not be an option at all for most of you, even on an occasional basis, but you may want to set up one or two alternative study sites.

In an empty classroom. Certainly an option at many colleges and perhaps some private high schools, it is an interesting idea mainly because so few students have ever thought of it!

At your job. Whether you're a student working part-time or fully employed and going to school part-time, you may be able to make arrangements to use an empty office, even during regular office hours, perhaps after everyone has left (depending on how much your boss trusts you). If you're in junior high or high school and a parent, friend or relative works nearby, you may be able to work from after school until closing time at their workplace.

How to stay focused on your studies

Whatever location you choose as your "study base", how you then set up your study area can affect your ability to stay focused and, if you aren't careful, seriously inhibit quality study time. If you find yourself doodling and dawdling more than diagramming and deciphering, consider these solutions:

Create a work environment in which you're *comfortable.* The size, style and placement of your desk, chair and lighting may all affect how easily (or poorly) you're distracted from the work at hand. Take the time to design the area that's perfect for you. Needless to say, anything that you know will distract you—a girlfriend's picture, a radio or TV, whatever, should disappear from your study area.

Turn up the lights. Subtle, recessed lighting may be beautiful in a living room, but it is probably not highly effective for really concentrated study. Experiment with the placement and intensity of lighting in your study area until you find what works for you, both in terms of comfort and as a means of staying awake and focused.

Set some rules. Let family, relatives and especially friends know how important your studying is and that specific hours are inviolate. Most people invariably call when you're right in the middle of something; by the time you get off the phone, you have to start over again. What a waste of precious study time!

Take the breaks you need. Don't follow some parent's or teacher's well-intentioned but bogus advice about how long you should study before taking a break. Take the breaks when *you* need to. If you're tired and just going through the motions, you're wasting time, even if your last break was 15 minutes ago. Take another and psyche yourself up for the next round!

Fighting tiredness and boredom

You've chosen the best study spot and no one could fault you on its set-up. So how come you're still mimicking a hypnotist's tiredness or boredom despite your best efforts to stay focused, help is on the way:

Take a nap. What a concept! When you're too tired to study, take a short nap to revive yourself. The key is to maximize that nap's effect, and *that* means keeping it short—20 minutes is ideal, 40 minutes absolute maximum. After that, you go into another phase of sleep and you may well wake even more tired than before. If you can't take such short naps, train yourself to do so.

Have a drink. A little caffeine won't harm you—a cup of coffee or tea, a glass of soda. Just be careful not to mainline it—caffeine's "wake up" properties seem to reverse when you reach a certain level, making you far more tired than you were!

Turn down the heat. You needn't build an igloo out back, but too warm a room will leave you dreaming of sugarplums.

Shake a leg. Or anything else that peps you up. Go for a walk, high step around the kitchen, do jumping jacks—even mild physical exertion will give you an immediate lift.

Change your study schedule. Presuming you have some choice here, find a way to study when *you* are normally more awake and/or most efficient.

The pharaohs wouldn't approve

Now I'll tell you about the Inverted Pyramid Theory I mentioned earlier in the book.

The top is very wide, the bottom is very narrow. This is symbolic of the way you should study for a test. Begin with all possible materials (all notes, book chapters, workbooks, audio tapes, etc.) and briefly review everything to see what you need to spend time with and what you can put aside.

I also call this separating the wheat from the chaff. The wheat is the edible good stuff that's taken from the field and turned into Chocolate Sugar Munchies. The chaff stays behind. The chaff was important at one time but it no longer is needed. The same is true of some of the material you've gathered for this next test. Now try this:

1. Gather all the material you have been using for the course: books, workbooks, handouts, notes, homework, previous tests and papers.

2. Compare the contents with the material you will be tested on and ask yourself: What exactly do I need to review for this test?

3. Select the material for review. Reducing the pile of books and papers will be a psychological aid— suddenly, it seems as if you will have enough time and energy to study for the test.

4. Photocopy and complete the Pre-Test Organizer on pages 124 and 125. Consider carefully the "Material to be covered" section on the second page.

   Be specific. The more detailed you are, the better job you'll do in reviewing all the areas that you should know. This exercise will help you *quantify* what you need to do. Instead of wandering aimlessly through your materials, you will have told yourself just where this information is.

5. As you review the material and conclude that you know it for the test, put a bold check mark on the

"OK" line. You are, to use my example, inverting the pyramid or shrinking the amount of material you need to study.

And you have time not only to spend on the stuff that's giving you grief, but to seek out other sources (fellow students, the teacher, the library, etc.) and get to the heart of the matter.

6. By the time the test is given, you should have reduced the "pyramid" to nothing. Take the test and do well!

You want to read it all again?

You neither have the time nor a valid reason to reread all the material. You *do* need to skim and scan it to pull out the essence and remind yourself of the main points.

Skimming is reading fast for an overview, for general information. Scanning is reading fast to find specifics. Both emphasize "fast" and "reading." You don't flip the pages of the book so quickly that you get a chill from the breeze. But you don't start reading the book all over again either.

Look at what you've underlined and highlighted. Look at boldfaced and italicized words, subheads, captions, questions— all in all, the "meat" of the chapter.

You're going to use the same reading methods with the other study material, including your notes. Probably your notes, however, should receive the most careful attention since they will reflect the teacher's lectures and her viewpoints and biases, as well as key buzzwords.

You don't want to obsess on your notes, but you can make notes from your notes as you study for the test. What I like to do is pull out of the notes the central ideas of the material being tested, sort of getting the *super*wheat out of the wheat.

The way of all flash

You probably remember flash cards from elementary school. On one side was a picture, on the other a word. Or one side held a definition ("Someone who studies bugs"), and the other the word being defined ("entomologist").

Flash cards are one of my favorite ways to test myself. They also work well with two people studying together or with a group. They work well for studying vocabulary, short answers, definitions, matching ("Boise" and "potato"), even true and false.

No person is an island

Don't face the Huguenots alone. Or even the periodic table of the elements. Share *your* knowledge while you benefit from the knowledge of a handful of other students in the same class. In other words, form a study group.

Try, if you can, to study with others who are at your level or slightly above. I say, *slightly* above. If you're a solid C and they're easy-A people, you won't connect. You'll want to review information they'll agree to skip. (And the opposite will happen to *you* if you choose people too far below you.)

Study groups can be organized in a variety of ways. Each member could be assigned primary responsibility for a single class, including preparing detailed notes from lectures and discussion groups. If supplementary reading is recommended but not required, that person could be responsible for doing all such reading and preparing detailed summaries.

(The extra work you will thus have to do in one class will be offset by the extra work others will be doing for you.)

Alternatively, everybody can be responsible for his or her own notes, but the group could act as an ad hoc discussion group, refining your understanding of key points, working on problems, questioning each other, practicing for tests, etc.

Even if you find only one or two other students willing to work with you, such cooperation will be invaluable, especially in preparing for major exams.

I suggest four students minimum, probably six maximum. You want to ensure everyone gets a chance to participate as much as they want while maximizing the collective knowledge and wisdom of the group.

While group members needn't be best friends, they shouldn't be overtly hostile to one another, either. Seek diversity of experience, demand common dedication. Avoid a group in which you're the "star"—at least until you flame out during the first exam.

Decide early on if you're forming a study group or a social group. If the latter, don't pretend it's the former. If the former, don't just invite your friends and informally sit around discussing your teachers for an hour a week.

Make meeting times and assignments formal and rigorous. Consider rigid rules of conduct. Shake out the non-serious students early. You don't want anyone who is working as little as possible but hoping to take advantage of *your* hard work.

However you organize, clearly decide—early—the exact requirements and assignments of each student. Again, you never want the feeling to emerge that one or two of you are trying to "ride the coattails" of the others.

Play it again, Mr. Sam

If you have access to old exams written by the same teacher, especially if they cover the same material you're going to be tested on, use them also for review.

Chances are the very same questions will *not* appear again. But the way the test is prepared, the kinds of questions, the emphasis on one kind of question over another (100 true/false, 50 multiple-choice and one—count 'em—one essay), will give you clues to what your own test will be about. At the same time, see if you can find anyone who had this teacher for this class last year or last semester. Can they give you any advice, tips, hints or warnings?

Once you've discovered the type of test facing you, you want to figure out what's going to be *on* it (and, hence, what you need to study). Remember, it's rarely, if ever, "everything."

In general, take the time to eliminate from consideration, with the possible exception of a cursory review, material you are convinced is simply not important enough to be included on an upcoming test. This will automatically give you more time to concentrate on those areas you are sure *will* be included.

Then create a "To Study" sheet for each test. On it, list specific books to review, notes to recheck, specific topics, principles, ideas and concepts to go over, etc. Then just check off each item as you study it. This method will minimize procrastination, logically organize your studying and give you on-going "jolts" of accomplishment as you complete each item.

Mnemonics and other words

What is that word, anyway? It refers to the practice of reducing a list of things you have to know to a simple way to remember them for the test. Warning: Some of these may stick with you for life. Here's an example:

Let's say you have to memorize the Seven Deadly Sins. (I said memorize them, not practice them.) I know—if you have one more list to learn, you'll scream. So make it a game, and make it easy to remember for the test.

"Sloth" is one of the seven. Think of lying around the house, having breakfast with a friend (instead of taking tests, going to class and all that). "Eggs pal" is your answer. The letters stand for the seven sins: In order, they are envy, greed, gluttony, sloth, pride, anger and lust.

You can also get pretty silly by making up associations that will help you remember a list of items or several matching pairs. It's more fun—and probably more successful—than memorizing long lists of facts for those times that you just need to know the information but you won't need it for the rest of your life.

An example of an association would be as follows: "I cry 'cause you gonna go, and Low Mate go to a free town with sarah alone." (Put a calypso beat to it.)

This beautifully crafted sentence contains clues to the answer to the following: "Match the following African countries with their capital cities."

Ghana	Freetown
Togo	Accra
Sierra Leone	Lome

Yes, of course, it's reaching. That's how associations work.

But suppose you couldn't remember which city went with which country. Or which political movement went with which social reformer. Or whatever. Use a "silly" way to hold the information together long enough for you to avoid a "silly" grade on the test.

All teachers are not equal (or fair or nice or...)

In an ideal world, all teachers would be filled with knowledge they eagerly and expertly shared with their students. Their lectures would be exciting (and brief). And their tests would be fair and accurate measurements of what the students should have learned.

Before you tell me about pigs flying, let me say that, in spite of the criticism schools and teachers have been getting for years, there are a lot of teachers out there like that. If you don't think you've had one yet, your turn is coming up.

In the meantime, though, let's consider Weird Al (or Weird Alice.) His personality may come out, unfortunately, when he writes and grades his tests. If you're lucky, you'll be forewarned by his former students so that you can be prepared as much as possible.

Watch for these danger signs. Even if he never seems to know when the next test will be, try to get that answer out of him. (Believe me, you want to ask. It's better to discover that it's a week from Thursday *today* rather than finding out a week from Wednesday.)

If he says he doesn't know what the test will cover, keep asking him. Also ask what types of questions will be on the test (true/false, multiple choice, essays, etc.) and what percentage of the test will be devoted to each. By your questions, you are helping him shape the test in his mind, and giving him the information he needs to give back to you.

Once you've taken the test, check your corrected test paper carefully. (This is true in any course, but here it's even more important.) If a right answer was marked wrong, let him know. If the question is too ambiguous and your answer could be right as well as the one *he* says is right, let him know.

And now, h-e-e-r-r-e's the SAT-I!

Well, you did it. You registered to take the SAT-I—the *new* one, for gosh sakes—and the Day of Reckoning is approaching.

While I'll share some specifics on taking any test, including the "new" SAT, in the next few chapters, for right now just remember that any hours-long national standardized test requires a lot of the same skills and the same planning as any unit quiz, chapter test, mid-term or final.

"Ace" Any Test

Since the SAT-I is intended to test your general knowledge of many areas, rather than grill you on the details from Chapter 14 of your chemistry book, you can and you *cannot* study for it. You cannot study specific material. On the other hand, you have been studying for these standardized tests all your life.

This test will seek to find out what you know about a lot of different subjects. Some of the answers will come from knowledge you gained years before. Others will come from your ability to work out the problems right there, using techniques and knowledge you gained years ago—and some you gained this semester.

To prepare for any major standardized test—the SAT-I, ACT, GRE, GMAT, etc.—I have one big suggestion: Determine, based on your past test-taking experiences and your comfort levels, what your weak areas are. Do you continually and completely mess up essay questions? Do analogies spin you out of control? Do you freeze at the sight of an isosceles triangle?

Seek out teachers, librarians and school counselors who can guide you to samples of these kinds of questions. Ask your teachers and fellow students for advice on handling the areas you feel you are weak in, take the sample tests, then work on evaluating how you did. Keep testing yourself and keep evaluating how you are doing.

Get advice from students who say things like, "Analogies? Piece of cake!" Find out if they really can do them easily and get tips from them (and from what I say in the following chapters).

Also, a good, solid review of basic math and English will be valuable. If geometry is not your strong suit, find a book that contains lists of the fundamentals and spend time reviewing information that you will be expected to exercise on the SAT-I. Do the same with the other subject areas to be tested. If your library doesn't have such materials, get advice from teachers or from the counseling office.

What's new about the "new" SAT-I?

As of March, 1994, students will no longer take the SAT; now they must prepare for the SAT-I. The Achievement Tests are also renamed—they are now called the "SAT-II." So what's really new?

Contrary to previous reports, *an essay is not part of the regular SAT-I* test. There *is* an essay on the SAT-II Writing Test (which is *not* required).

Not all questions will be multiple choice. Out of 60 SAT-1 math questions, for example, 10 will offer no choices at all. You have to come up with the right answer on your own.

Say good-by to antonyms, which are no longer included. However, the vocabulary used in the sentence completion questions, analogics and reading comprehension selections will be more difficult.

Scoring for each section (verbal and math) still ranges from 200 to 800, but the number of verbal questions counted in your score has been reduced from 85 to 78. Seventy-five minutes is still allotted for that section (and 75 minutes for the 60 math questions, unchanged in number from previous years).

However, according to the March 10, 1994 issue of *USA Today,* the average 1995 score will jump 98 points (from 424 on the verbal and 478 on the math to 500 on each). How can that happen, especially since the average for 1993 was 54 points *lower* than 1969? Are students predicted to be so much smarter? No, the College Board has merely decided to set the midpoint at 500 (which is, of course, halfway between 200 and 800!). Since this is merely a change in scale, the relative ranking of students won't be affected at all. While this will make everything look better, it will naturally make life difficult for anyway attempting to draw comparisons between students' 1995 performance and that from previous years.

There will still be a 30-minute experimental section in either verbal or math. *These questions and answers don't count in any score.*

Say hello to calculators, which can now be brought and used. According to the SAT experts I spoke with, there will *not* be any questions designed to be *easier* to solve with calculators. Indeed, they are designed to be solved just as quickly (and, in some cases, *more* quickly) with*out* a calculator.

Watch those guesses—There's a 1/4 point penalty for an incorrect answer to a question offering five answer choices, a 1/3 point penalty for one offering four choices. Strategize accordingly!

To be coached or not to be coached?

Should you take one of those SAT preparation courses? Is it worth the money, the time, the effort, the bother?

The answer is a definite "maybe." It depends on a handful of factors: First of all, ask others for recommendations. Listen closely to why they liked or disliked a particular course (their reasons may not match your reasons—tread carefully here). Ask particularly about each course's effectiveness and results.

Decide if you have the time and money to take a course. If you do, which kind do you want? There are coaching classes taught by humans, but there are also books/cassette tapes combos and computer programs. Ask your school counseling office for recommendations, also. (They may even have copies of some of the programs.) If you don't have the money, ask about available financial aid and ways to reduce tuition.

Evaluate the professionalism of whatever course you're considering. How good are their materials? Do they look complete and professionally prepared, or will you be given a sheaf of badly photocopied forms and a ratty binder? Can you attend one meeting free to get a feel for the procedures? Will they furnish you with the resumes of your instructors? Will those instructors be accessible outside of class?

Finally, are there any money-back guarantees? The best companies—in this or any field—stand behind their product, even if that means giving full refunds to dissatisfied customers.

There's method in their madness—I think

The standardized-test coaching programs should deal with two areas. I'll call them Method and Content.

Method is the study of *how* to take a test, specifically how to take the SAT-I, ACT, GRE, whatever. That portion of the course will cover much of the same material that you're reading in this book, especially the material we're going to look at in the next two chapters.

Content deals with practicing the sort of stuff that's going to be on the specific test you're taking: vocabulary words, math problems, essay questions, analogies and so on.

The two areas overlap, of course. When you work math problems there are "methods" you utilize to get the answer, just as there is "content."

Practicing for standardized tests by answering questions that are similar in content to what you will later be tested on is a valuable exercise, but it's only half the equation. The other half is the feedback you get from your coach (or teacher, counselor, or fellow students) on how you did, what you did, and why you did what you did. It won't do you any good to keep messing up on analogies, for example, if you can't figure out how to do them right.

Chapter Five

ESSAY TESTS: WRITE ON!

"There is no room for the impurities of literature in an essay." —Virginia Woolf (1882-1941)

"Essay: ...an irregular indigested piece." —Samuel Johnson (1709-1784)

Just be glad that dear Virginia isn't grading *your* essay.

Essay questions. Some students love them. Some hate them. It's hard to feel indifferent about those lengthy sections that can take up pages and pages of a test—and pages and pages of an answer booklet.

Personally, I think *all* "objective" tests are harder than an essay test. Why? An objective test of any kind gives the teacher much more latitude, even the option of focusing *only* on the obscurest details (which, granted, only the truly sadistic would do). As a result, it's much more difficult to eliminate areas or topics when studying for such a test. It's also rare to be given a choice—answer any 25 out of 50—whereas you may often be given, for example, five essay questions and have to choose only three. This greatly increases the odds that even sporadic studying will have at least given you some understanding about one or two of the questions, whereas you may be lost on a 100-question true-false test.

Why else did I like essay tests? Less could go wrong on an essay test—there were only three or four questions to read, not a hundred potential *mis*reads. I could think of a few questions, not hundreds. I could take the time to organize (a strength) and would probably get extra points for good spelling, grammar and writing (another strength). It's also easier to budget time among three or four essay questions than among 150 multiple-choice.

Whether you love or hate essays, there are some important pointers to ensure you a least score better on them.

Of course you know this, but...

Really advanced schools with big budgets provide typewriters or computers for their students so they can write essays in the classroom. But we can't all have 90210 as our ZIP code. The rest of you will have to work with a pen.

First of all, make sure it's a pen. A good one. One that you're comfortable with. If you hate ball-points and swear by felt-tips, then go for it. Actually, go for *them*. Only someone who wants a bad grade shows up with one pen. Of course, it will run out, begin to leak, break or all of the above if you have only one. If you have two (or, for the truly superstitious, three or more) then, of course, the first pen will be working like that annoying drum-beating rabbit when your grandchildren are taking the SAT-CCXXVIII on Mars.

Think before you ink

Approach essay questions the same way you would a paper. While you can't check your textbook or go to the library to do research, the facts, ideas, comparisons, etc. you need are in your own cerebral library—your mind.

Don't ever, *ever* begin writing the answer to an essay question without a little "homework" first. I don't care if you're the school's prize-winning journalist.

First, really look at the question. Are you sure you know what it's asking? What are the verbs? Don't "describe" when it calls for you to "compare and contrast." Don't "explain" when it tells you to "argue." Underline the verbs. (See pages 81 and 82 for a list of the most-used such verbs in essay tests and what each is instructing you to do.)

Then sit back a minute and think about what you're going to say. Or less than a minute, depending on how much time you have, but *don't* just start writing.

Here's the step-by-step way to answer every essay question:

Step One: On a blank sheet of paper, write down all the facts, ideas, concepts, etc. you feel should be included in your answer.

Step Two: Organize them in the order in which they should appear. You don't have to rewrite your notes into an outline—just number each note according to where you want to place it.

Step Three: Compose your first paragraph, working on it just as hard as I suggested you do on your papers. It should summarize and introduce the key points you will make. *This is where superior essay answers are made or unmade.*

Step Four: Write your essay.

Step Five: Reread your essay and, if necessary, add points left out, correct spelling, grammar, etc. Also watch for a careless omission that could cause serious damage—such as leaving out a "not", making the point opposite of the one you wanted to.

If there is a particular fact you know is important and should be included but you just don't remember it, guess if you can. Otherwise, just leave it out and do the best you can. If the rest of your essay is well-thought-out and organized and clearly communicates all the other points that should be included, I doubt most teachers will mark you down too severely for such an omission.

Remember: Few teachers will be impressed by length. A well-organized, well-constructed, specific answer to their question will always get you a better grade than "shot-gunning"— writing down everything you know in the faint hope that you will actually hit something. Worry less about the specific words and more about the information. Organize your answer to a fault and write to be understood, not to impress. Better to use shorter sentences, paragraphs and words—and be clear and concise—than to let the teacher fall into a clausal nightmare from which he may never emerge (and neither will your "A"!).

If you don't have the faintest clue what the question means, ask. If you still don't have any idea of the answer—and I mean *zilch*—leave it blank. Writing down everything you think you know about the supposed subject in the hopes that one or two things will actually have something to do with the question is, in my mind, a waste of everyone's time. Better to allocate the time you would waste to other parts of the test and do a better job on those.

The best-organized beats the best-written

While I think numbering your notes is as good an organizational tool as jotting down a complete outline, there is certainly nothing wrong with fashioning a quick outline. Not one with Roman numerals—this outline will consist of a simple list of abbreviated words, scribbled on a piece of scrap paper or in the margin of your test booklet. The purpose of this outline is the same as those fancy ones: to make sure you include everything you need and want to say—in order.

Let's suppose this is the essay question: "Discuss the effects of Mabel Dodge Luhan on the cultural and social life of Taos, New Mexico." Your outline might look like this:

1. intro —ovrvw MDL on T
   —brt a&w, stay

2. social —top dog
   —salon
   —a&w brt a&w
   —a. scene

3. cult. —hist. Sp/NA
   —hse/gr

4. conc. —wht lke?
   —thks her
   —incr.

Notice that almost no words are written out completely. After all, no one is going to grade this outline. In fact, no one else is even going to *see* it. Let me write out the whole outline for you. You won't do this, of course, but I want you to see, before you read the actual essay, what I had in mind when I wrote out those hieroglyphics above.

1. Introduction
   A. Overview of Mabel Dodge Luhan's influence on Taos.
   B. She brought artists and writers to visit, some of whom then moved there.

2. Social effects
   A. Mabel was the head of "society" in Taos.
   B. She created a "salon" atmosphere in her home.
   C. Her friends, the famous artists and writers, brought other artists and writers to Taos—and to Mabel.

3. Cultural effects
   A. Historic aspects, especially the promotion of the Native American and Spanish cultures.
   B. Her own house and grave today are part of the historic/cultural scene.

4. Conclusion
   A. Taos wouldn't be the same without her.
   B. Thanks to her, it's a bustling town today filled with artistic residents and visitors.
   C. The cultural and social scene—which she developed—continues to increase in numbers and importance.

You are going to start off strong, with bold statements that begin the discussion and refer directly to the question. This introduction will put Mabel in context.

In this second part of the outline ("social effects"), you begin to deal with the gut issue of the essay. There have been whole books written about Mabel, so you aren't going to be able to tell everything about her in one comparatively short essay. Nor, more importantly, should you. The question, after all, doesn't say, "Tell as much as you can cram into one blue book about Mabel Dodge Luhan." No, it asks for specific, limited, restricted and definite answers.

I might as well make my "quality, not quantity" speech here, too. I hope you write well. It's important. But excellent writing, even pages and pages of it, will not get you an excellent grade unless you have the quality—meaning hard-hitting, incisive, direct answers.

Again, most teachers won't fall for the beautifully crafted, empty answer. Don't depend on your good looks or your command of the subjunctive to get you by. Go home and study.

But, back to the second item on your outline. You will write about the social effects—one-half of the question, at this point. Give examples and be as specific as you can. If the teacher has provided certain information that you dutifully copied into your notes, be sure to include this information here. If the teacher was really enthusiastic about something and referred to it a number of times, take the hint—and take your pen and give that information back in your own words.

Think of the introduction and the conclusion as the bread in a sandwich, with the information in between as the hamburger, lettuce, tomato and pickle. Everything is necessary for it all to hang together, but the main attraction is going to be what's between the slices.

Now, let's see how I'd write this essay:

The Effects of Mabel Dodge Luhan on the
Cultural and Social Life of Taos, New Mexico

Mabel Dodge Luhan had an extraordinary effect on the life of the little mountain town of Taos, New Mexico. From the time she arrived in 1917 until her death in 1962, Mabel was the social and cultural life of the town. She not only brought her own personality to the artists' colony, but numerous artists and writers to visit Taos as well. Some of them remained in the area for the rest of their lives.

The gatherings of these famous people—D.H. Lawrence, Georgia O'Keeffe, Greta Garbo, Leopold Stokowski and others—in Mabel's house served as a kind of "salon" where important members of the American and European artistic communities met, discussed each other's work, and spread the word about Taos and Mabel when they returned to New York, California or Europe. Their enthusiasm helped bring even more famous people to visit Taos.

The social scene in Taos centered on Mabel. Because she was a personal friend of most of the people who visited her, as well as being wealthy, domineering and extremely active, she reigned as the head of the social order in the town during her entire lifetime. The other prominent members of the community—the artists, the wealthy ranchers, the merchants—all formed a pecking order beneath her.

Mabel's support of the artistic community earlier in this century helped spread the fame of these artists—and increased the sale of their works. The prominence of Taos as an artists' colony, thanks in part to Mabel, encouraged even more artists to move to Taos, which, in turn, increased the number of visitors who came to town to buy art or simply to look at it—while spending money at the restaurants, hotels, bars and gift shops. This trend has continued—Taos today is a major art center in the U.S. with dozens of art galleries and tourist-related shops.

The historic, as well as artistic, aspects of Taos were promoted by Mabel. Her artist friends painted people, places and events connected to the local Spanish and Native American cultures. These paintings, and the media attention given to the historic aspects of the town, helped spread the fame of Taos.

Today, Mabel's house and her grave, in the historic Kit Carson Cemetery, are two of many attractions that tourists visit when they come to town.

It is difficult to imagine what Taos would be like today had Mabel Dodge Luhan not taken up residence there in 1917. For 45 years, her promotion of the little town gave it worldwide fame. Artists, historians, writers and tourists began to visit Taos. Each year, the number of visitors—and social and cultural events, art galleries and historic tours—increases, thanks to the influence of Mabel Dodge Luhan.

There. You may never write about Mabel (all of the above is true, by the way), but if you "translate" the outline/ essay exercise to a topic you are studying (the French Revolution, Chicago architecture or the influence of the hot dog on National League batting averages), you can do the same.

Give me some space, man

Plan ahead. Write your essay on every other line and on one side of the paper or page only. This will give you room to add or correct anything without having to write it so small that it is illegible and, therefore, doesn't earn you any credit. It also helps keep the whole paper neater and, psychologically, that should help you get a slightly better grade. Most teachers won't admit it, but they will give a few more points to tests that are neat, clean and done with a good pen. Think about it. How many slobs do you know who are "A" students?

Proof it!

Budget your time so that you can go back over your essay, slowly, and correct any mistakes or make any additions. Check your spelling, punctuation, grammar and syntax. (And if you don't know what that is, find out. You'll need to know for the SAT.) It would be a shame for you to write a beautiful essay and lose points because you had those kinds of errors.

When you're done, you're done...almost

Resist the temptation to leave the room or turn in your paper before you absolutely have to. Imagine the pain of sitting in the cafeteria, while everyone else is back in the room, continuing to work on the test, and you suddenly remember what else you could have said to make your essay really sparkle. But it's too late!

Take the time at the end of the test to review not only your essay answers, but your other answers as well. Make sure all words and numbers are readable. Make sure you have matched the right question and the right answer. Even make sure you didn't miss a whole section by turning over a page too quickly. Make sure you can't, simply *can't*, add anything more to any of the essay answers. Make sure. Make sure. Make sure.

If you're out of time are you out of luck?

While you should have carefully allocated sufficient time to complete each essay before you started working on the first, things happen. And you may find yourself with two minutes left and one essay to go. What do you do? As quickly as possible, write down everything you think should be included in your answer and number each point in the order in which you would have written it. If you then have time to reorganize your notes into a better-organized outline, do so. Many teachers will give you at least partial credit (some very near *full* credit) if your outline contains all the information the answer was supposed to. It will at least show you knew a lot about the subject and were capable of outlining a reasonable response.

One of the reasons you may have left yourself with insufficient time to answer one or more questions is because you knew too darned much about the previous question(s). And you wanted to make sure the teacher *knew* you knew, so you wrote...and wrote...and wrote...until you ran out of time. Be careful—some teachers throw in a relatively general question that, if you wanted to, you could write about until next Wednesday. In that case, they aren't testing your knowledge of the whole subject as much as your ability to *edit* yourself, to organize and summarize the *important* points. Just remember that no matter how fantastic your answer to any one essay, it is going to get 1/5 the overall score (presuming five questions)— that is, 20 points, never more, even if you turn in a publishable book manuscript. Meanwhile, 80 points are waiting for you.

If you've mastered the tips and techniques in this chapter, you will, from now on, "be like Ron": You'll positively drool when you see a test that's nothing but essays!

Common Instructional Verbs on Essay Tests

Compare   Examine two or more objects, ideas, people, etc. and note similarities and differences.

Contrast   Compare to highlight differences.

Criticize   Judge and discuss the merits and faults of (similarly, **critique**)

Define   Explain or identify the nature or essential qualities of.

Describe   Convey the appearance, nature, attributes, etc. of something

Discuss   Consider or examine by argument, comment, etc.; debate; explore solutions.

Enumerate List various events, things, descriptions, ideas, etc.

Evaluate   Appraise the worth of an idea, comment, etc. and justify your conclusion.

Explain   Make the meaning of something clear, plain, intelligible and/or understandable.

Illustrate   Use specific examples or analogies to clarify or explain.

Interpret   Give the meaning of something by paraphrase, by translation or by an explanation based on personal opinion.

Justify   Defend or uphold a statement, decision or conclusion.

Narrate   Similar to **describe**, but only applicable to something that happens in time. Hence, it is to recount the occurrence of something, usually by giving details of events in the order in which they occurred.

"Ace" Any Test

Outline Do a general sketch, account or report, indicating only the main features of a book, subject or project.

Prove Establish the truth or genuineness of by evidence or argument. (In math, verify validity by mathematical demonstration.)

Relate Give an account of happenings, events and/or circumstances, usually to establish association, connections or relationships.

Review Survey a topic, occurrence or idea, generally but critically.

State Present the facts concisely and clearly.

Summarize State in concise form, omitting examples, analogies and details.

Trace Follow the course, development or history of an occurrence, idea, etc.

Chapter Six

OBJECTIVE TESTS: LEARN TO DISCRIMINATE AND ELIMINATE

Some people prefer objective tests to essays. After all, in multiple-choice questions, the answer is staring you in the face (and sticking out its tongue at you, if you want to know the truth). You just have to be able to figure out which one it is.

In this chapter, we're going to look at the different types of objective tests and some of the methods to use to answer each type, based primarily on "the process of elimination." If you learn nothing else from this chapter, learn this: The process of elimination has saved many a person from failure. It may just save you.

Place sprocket A into dovetail XY using tube C-14

A very key point of preparation I should have mentioned earlier: Read and understand the directions. Otherwise, you could seemingly do everything *right,* but not follow your teacher's explicit directions, in which case everything's *wrong.*

If you're supposed to check off *every* correct answer to each question in a multiple choice test—and you're assuming only *one* answer to each question is correct—you're going to miss a lot of answers!

If you're to pick one essay question out of three, or two out of five, that's a lot different than trying to answer every one. You won't do it. And even if you do, the teacher will probably only grade the first two. Because you needed to allocate enough time to do the other three, it's highly doubtful your first two answers will be so detailed and so perfect that they will be able to stand alone.

Are the questions or sections weighted? Some tests may have two, three or more sections, some of which count for very little—10 or 20 percent of your final score—while one, usually a major essay, may be more heavily weighted—50 percent or more of your grade. This should drastically alter the time you spend on each section.

And be aware of time. Again, if questions or sections are weighted, you will want to allow extra time for those that count the most. Better to do a superior job on the two sections that count for 90 percent of the score and whip through the 10-percent section as the teacher is collecting booklets.

I know students who, before they write a single answer, look through the entire test and break it down into time segments—allocating 20 minutes for section one, 40 for section two, etc. Even on multiple choice tests, they count the total number of questions, divide by the time allotted and set "goals" on what time they should reach question 10, question 25, etc.

I never did it. But I think it's a great idea—if it turns out to be a workable organizational tool for you and not just one more layer of pressure.

If there are pertinent facts or formulas you're afraid you'll forget, I also think it's a good idea to write them down somewhere in your test booklet before you do anything else. It won't take much time and it could save you some serious memory jogs later.

A guess in time

Will you be penalized for guessing? The teacher, for example, may inform you that you will earn two points for every correct answer but *lose* one point for every incorrect one. This will certainly affect whether you guess or skip the question—or, at the very least, how many potential answers you feel you need to eliminate before the odds of guessing are in your favor.

There is usually nothing wrong with guessing, unless, of course, you know wrong answers will be penalized. Even then, as I've pointed out, guessing is not necessarily wrong. The question is how *much* to guess.

If there is no penalty for wrong answers, you should *never* leave an answer blank. But you should also do everything you can to increase your odds of getting it right. If every multiple-choice question gives you four possible answers, you have a 25-percent chance of being right (and, of course, a 75-percent chance of being wrong) each time you have to guess.

But if you can eliminate a single answer—one you are reasonably certain cannot be right—your chances of being correct are 33 percent.

And, of course, if you can get down to a choice between two answers, it's just like flipping a coin: 50-50. In the long run, you will guess as many right as wrong.

Even if there is a penalty for guessing, I would probably pick one answer if I had managed to increase my chances of getting the right one to 50-50.

"Ace" Any Test

Presuming that you've managed to eliminate one or more answers but are still unsure of the *correct* answer—and have no particular way to eliminate further—here are some real insider tips to make your "guess" more "educated":

- If two answers sound alike, choose one of them.
- If the answers that are left to a mathematical question cover a broad range, choose the number in the middle.
- If two quantities are very close, choose one of them.
- If two numbers differ only by a decimal point (and the others aren't close), choose one of them (Example: 2.3, 40, 1.5, 6, 15; I'd go for either 1.5 or 15. If I could at least figure out from the question where the decimal point should go, even better!)
- If two answers to a mathematical problem *look* alike— either formulas or shapes—choose one of them.

Remember: This is not the way to ace a test, just some tried-and-true ways to increase your guessing power *when you have absolutely nothing else to go on and nothing else to do.* And please don't write me nasty letters if you chose one of two similar-sounding words and they were both the wrong answer. First, there are no guarantees when you guess. And second, teachers read these books, too!

Eliminate the obvious and sort-of obvious

Suppose the question was as follows: "The first U.S. President to appoint a woman to the Cabinet was (A) Franklin D. Roosevelt, (B) Herbert Hoover, (C) Abraham Lincoln or (D) Jimmy Carter."

Heck if I know, you may be saying. Most likely, you can get this down to two choices pretty quickly. Why? Think about women's rights and the role of women in society. OK, that's long enough.

You're absolutely correct to eliminate, right away, Abraham Lincoln. It wasn't that he was a bad guy; you just have to remember that women didn't even have the right to vote at that time, and laws and customs kept women from doing most of what they are doing today. The likelihood of a woman being in the President's Cabinet in the 1860s is very, very, very slim.

Let's now go to the other extreme. You may be fuzzy on who was in Jimmy Carter's Cabinet (he may have been fuzzy, too), but even if you are too young to remember Carter, you're guessing that he was recent enough not to be the first president to appoint women in that role. Score another point for the process of elimination.

Now comes the hard part. If you have any knowledge of history, and I hope you do, you know that the two remaining choices were, at least, presidents during the 20th century...in other words, after women got the right to vote. (Women could have served in the Cabinet without the right to vote, but it isn't very logical, is it? That's why I'm pegging my answer to that historic decision.)

You may not be able to get past this choice. But, even if you can't and you blindly select one or the other, your chance of selecting the correct answer is one out of two. Even if your teacher deducts points, I would go ahead and put down (A) or (B).

Those of you who know a little more about history than average are going to be able to figure it out by remembering that Roosevelt was a very different sort of President. He was loved or hated for his dramatic changes in government, while Hoover was the poster boy for The Status Quo Society. If that difference in their styles and actions comes to mind, then you'd be 100 percent correct to choose FDR.

Check it out, check it out!

Use this process of elimination for all types of objective questions. Depending on whether you can eliminate any of the answers and whether you feel you can "afford" to lose the points will help you decide how to answer the question.

If there is time during a test for you to come back to questions and look at them one more time, go ahead and put a line through the answers you know can't be correct. That will simply save you time. You will ignore the answers that are struck out and concentrate on the ones that remain. A small point, but it can save you several seconds.

What about going back, rechecking your work, and changing a guess? How valid was that first guess? Surprisingly, perhaps, statistics show it was probably pretty darned good (presuming you had some basis for guessing in the first place). So good that you should *only* change it *if:*

- It really *was* just a wild guess and, upon further thought, you conclude your "guess" answer really should be eliminated (in which case your next guess is, at least, not quite so wild).
- You remembered something that changes the odds of your guess completely (or the answer to a later question helped you figure out the answer to this one!).
- You miscalculated on a math problem.
- You misread the question (didn't notice a "not", an "always" or some other important qualifier, for example).

Get visual

Throughout a test, don't miss an opportunity to draw a picture for yourself if this will help you understand the question and figure out the right answer.

I believe in being as visual as possible. If the question deals with any sort of cause-and-effect that has several steps in it, literally draw or write down those steps very quickly, using abbreviated words or symbols. It's like making a quick outline, as we discussed in the chapter on essay questions.

Putting it down like that may help you see any missing pieces, help you understand relationships between any of the parts and, thus, help you select the right answer.

And the answer is...!

Especially with multiple-choice answers, read the question, then try to guess the answer before you look at what's there. Very often, you'll be right—or at least you'll be close and you can begin the elimination process immediately.

14 tips for "Acing" multiple-choice tests

1. Be careful you don't read too much into questions. You can try to second-guess the test preparer, get too elaborate and ruin the answer.
2. Underline the key words.
3. If two choices are very similar, the answer is probably not either one of them.
4. If two choices are opposite, one of them is probably correct.
5. Don't go against your first impulse unless you are *sure* you were wrong. (Sometimes you're so smart you scare yourself.)
6. Check for negatives and other words that are there to throw you off. ("Which of the following is *not*....")
7. The answer is usually wrong if it contains "all, always, never or none." Usually.

8. The answer has a great chance of being right if it has "sometimes, probably or some."

9. When you don't know the right answer, look for the wrong one. Start *that* process rolling.

10. Don't eliminate an answer unless you actually know what every word means.

11. Read every answer (unless you are wildly guessing at the last minute and there's no penalty).

12. If it's a standardized test, consider transferring all the answers from one section to the answer sheet at once. This can save time. Just be careful: make sure you're putting each answer in the right place.

13. If you're supposed to read a long passage and then answer questions about it, read the questions *first*. That will tell you what you're looking for and *affect the way you read the passage*. If dates are asked for, circle all dates in the passage as you read. If you're looking for facts rather than conclusions, it will, again, change the way you read the passage. (And when you first read the question—but before you even look at the answer choices—decide what you think the answer is. If your answer is one of the choices you've been given, bingo!)

14. The longest and/or most complicated answer to a question is often correct—the test maker has been forced to add qualifying clauses or phrases to make that answer complete and unequivocal.

Analogies: Study : Succeed as Eat : ?

I may be a sick puppy, but I like analogies. In the heat of completing 30 of them on a test, I may have slight second thoughts, but I look upon them as incredible brain teasers.

Pause with me a minute while I practice a little pop psychology. Think of any of these tests, even the SAT, as a game. I don't mean you don't take it seriously. Of course you want to get the highest score or the best grade possible.

But look upon it as you might a sports event. It's a challenge. You've prepared mentally just as you would prepare physically for basketball or tennis. Why not look upon it in a positive sense, as a challenge for you to take on, to compete with yourself for the best possible outcome?

If you have that kind of attitude, you will remain in a better frame of mind prior to the test and during it, and you'll do better. End of sermon. Back to analogies.

Taking it all apart

To help you figure out the right answer in an analogy, write it out, or, at least, think it out. Suppose the question was as follows:

POLICE : ARREST
    (A) priest : church
    (B) doctor : prescribe
    (C) driver : sleep
    (D) lawyer : court

Begin by deciding what the relationship is between "police" and "arrest." First of all, what parts of speech are "police" and "arrest" in this example? If you're not suffering from too much heavy-metal music appreciation, you should come up with "noun : verb."

The correct answer is going to have the same relationship. Two of the answers, (B) and (C), are noun : verb. For "priest" to be considered, it would have to be something like "priest :

pray" or "priest : preach." Likewise, (D) would have to be something like "lawyer : practice" or "lawyer : sue".

So we've eliminated two of the four already. Look at the police example. What is the relationship between "police" and "arrest?" If you write or think it out, you'll come up with: "arrest is one thing police do as part of their job."

Which now seems correct? The doctor or the driver? If you substitute "doctor" and "prescribe" in the above sentence, doesn't that sound correct? But if you put "driver" and "sleep" in the same places, does it make sense? Not really. We assume that, at some point or other, all drivers sleep (at least we hope so as they are rapidly maneuvering us through traffic on the way home from school), but it isn't a part of their job.

Some samples for you to taste

Many of these basic principles apply to the other types of questions you'll find on an objective test. Matching one item with another, completing sentences, doing math problems, choosing the correct vocabulary word—all rely on:

1. (a) your prior knowledge gained from studying for this particular course
   (b) all the reading, studying and listening you've been doing for years
2. your common sense
3. your ability to eliminate as many as possible of the potential answers
4. paying close attention to and following directions

Let's run through an example of another type of question, this one involving antonyms (even though they're gone, thankfully, from the SAT-I):

MAMMOTH: (A) colossal
(B) minuscule
(C) perpendicular
(D) moderate

The test writer has thrown in (A) to see if you'll flub up and choose a synonym instead. Not exactly dirty pool, but a technique to watch for. And (C) is there as a kind of off-center joke. Huh? But some people think that, because it is so unusual, it must be right. Answer (D) is a variation on (A) in that it refers to size, but it's not the right size for the answer.

The correct answer must be (B), and it is. Even if you didn't know what "minuscule" meant, you should have been able to figure out that "mini" is tiny or little or as close to the opposite of "mammoth" as you're going to get here.

Comprehension questions

This is the portion of the test where you find a short essay, followed by several questions. You are supposed to find the answers to those questions in the essay.

Unlike the multiple-choice questions, where the answer is actually right in front of you, the answers to the essay questions may well be hidden in one fashion or another.

Not since third grade have you had an essay question that asks, "How old was Thomas Jefferson when he first went to Bloomingdale's?" and, lo and behold, back in the essay it clearly says, "Thomas Jefferson was 17 when he visited Bloomingdale's for the first time." Unfortunately for you, those questions went out with notes that said, "Do you love me? Yes or No!," and recess.

You're lucky if you get questions like, "How old was Thomas Jefferson when he became President?" and the essay says, "Thomas Jefferson ascended to the office of the President 33 years after his first election as a member of the Virginia House of Burgesses in 1768."

Buried somewhere else in the essay will be something like, "Jefferson, born 33 years before the Declaration of Independence, ..." Since you should know that the Declaration of Independence was written in 1776, you can figure out he was born in 1743 and that he became President in 1801. The rest is history.

Don't confuse me with facts

Look at that example again. Did it ever say the year of Jefferson's birth or the year he became President? Nope. It gave you, in two different places, enough information to figure it out.

At the same time, those terrible tricksters have thrown in enough dates and enough numbers to get people to write down "33" or "66" as the right answer. Also, they don't offer the information in strict chronological order—another way to mess you up.

This is where too little attention to detail can get a wrong answer on paper. Before you search for the answer, you need to decide what the question is.

Don't jump to conclusions so quickly that you grab the first number that you see. In fact, you can be pretty sure that any number that you see will *not* be the answer.

In the Jefferson example, you might have quickly scribbled down the following information just to get your bearings, and the correct answer:

1. 1776	**2.** 1768	**3.** 1801
- 33	+ 33	-1743
1743 birth	1801 Prez	58

Here's the method I recommend for answering comprehension questions:

1. Read the questions first. Consider them clues in a puzzle. You'll be alerted to what the essay is about so that you don't start "cold" with the first paragraph.
2. Slowly read the essay, keeping in mind the questions you've just read. Don't underline too much, but do underline conjunctions that change the direction of the sentence: however, although, nevertheless, yet, etc. Because of this shift, there is a good chance that this sentence will figure in one of the questions.

   For example, this sentence in the essay, "John Smith was the kind of writer who preferred writing over editing, *while* his wife Lois was interested in the latter over the former," might provide the answer to the question: "Did Lois Smith prefer writing or editing?" A too-careless glance back at the text will cause you to select "writing" as the answer.
3. Read the questions again. Then go back and forth, finding out the answer to the first one, the second one, etc. Don't skip around unless the first question is an absolute stumper. If you jump around too much, you'll get confused again and you won't answer any of the questions very completely or even correctly.

You're failing this test. True or false?

I think true-false tests are generally more insidious than multiple-choice, because the latter at least offers the correct answer, which you may well pick out without knowing it's correct.

That's the bad news.

The good news is that it's hard to beat 50-50 odds!

What can you do to increase your scores on true-false tests?

First of all, be more inclined to guess if you have to. After all, I encouraged you to guess on a multiple-choice test if you could eliminate enough wrong answers to get down to two, one of which is correct. Well, you're already there! So, unless you are being penalized for guessing, guess away! (And even if you are being penalized, you may well want to take a shot if you have the faintest clue of the correct answer.)

What tricks do test makers incorporate in true-false tests? Here are three to watch out for:

Two parts (statements) that *are* true (or, at least, *may* be true) linked in such a way that the *whole* statement becomes false. Example: "Since many birds can fly, they use stones to grind their food." Many birds *do* fly, and birds *do* swallow stones to grind their food. But a *causal relationship* (the word "since") between the two clauses makes the whole statement false.

The longer and/or more complicated a statement in a true-false test, the *less* likely it's true since *every clause* of it must be true (and there are so many chances for a single part of it to be false).

Few broad, general statements are true *without exception*. So always be on your guard when you see the words "all", "always", "no", "never" or other absolutes. As long as you can think of a *single* example which proves such a statement false, then it is false. But be wary: There are statements with such absolutes that *are* true; they are just rare.

Matching

Match the following countries with their capitals:

Thailand	Paris
Japan	Kuala Lumpur
France	Tokyo
Malaysia	Bangkok

Match the obvious ones first. Let's say you know Paris and Tokyo are the capitals of France and Japan, respectively. Look at the two remaining ones. Here's where common sense and good general knowledge will come in handy.

Because you probably get a lot of your world news from the radio and TV, you may well have heard the combos more than you've seen them. Go with the ones that "sound right." (In this case, Bangkok, Thailand and Kuala Lumpur, Malaysia.)

Sentence completions

Like many of the other kinds of problems, sentence completions can often be figured out by putting the question into context or into perspective. Here's an example:

"The hypnotist said to the man, 'You're very _____.'"

    (A) sleepy   (D) ill
    (B) rich   (E) busy
    (C) ugly

Quick. What do hypnotists do? What do they say (at least in the movies)? It has to be (A). Now, somewhere since the dawn of time, a hypnotist has said all of the other words. He may also have said, "Do you know what Spiro Agnew's doing now?" but that doesn't make the words right. We're looking for logic and common sense here.

Multiple-choice math

Process of elimination is important in finding the answers. There are some numbers to consider, also. For example, scan the problem below and see if you can figure out the answer without actually doing the math:

334 x 412 =
(A)   54,559
(B)   137,608
(C)   22,528
(D)   229,766

By performing one simple task, you can eliminate two of the possible answers. Multiply the last digits in each number (2 x 4). The answer must end in 8. So (A) and (D) have been eliminated...that fast!

Now, eyeball (B) and (C). Can you find the right answer quickly? Here you are doing educated guessing, known in math circles as "guesstimating." Look: 334 x 100 is 33,400. You should be able to do that without any tools. Therefore, (C) has to be wrong. You are left with (B).

Should you do the actual math to double-check your answer? I wouldn't. You know that (A) and (D) are wrong. Absolutely. You know from a quick ballpark multiplying that (C) is much too low. Mark (B) as the answer and move on.

Here are some other ways to better your score on math tests:

• Try to figure out what is being asked, what principles are involved, what information is important, what's not. Don't let extraneous data throw you off track.
• Whenever you can, "translate" formulas and numbers into words.
• Even if you're not particularly visual, pictures can often help. Try translating a particularly vexing math problem into a drawing or diagram.
• Play around. There often different paths to the same solution, or even equally valid solutions.

- When you are checking your calculations, try working *back*wards. I've found it an easier way to catch simple arithmetical errors.

The importance of words

No matter how much you study principles and examples, you will be lost if the words used in the test are simply not in *your* vocabulary. I could make the point, of course, that without a sufficient vocabulary, you won't be able to keep up with the principles anyway. Like reading itself, building a workable vocabulary is absolutely essential to doing well on any kind of test, since you are more likely to understand the directions, the questions and the possible answers.

Build your vocabulary as much as you can. Read good books. Listen to people with large vocabularies. Write down the words you don't know and become friendly with them. The more words you know, the better you can play the "process of elimination" game and the better score you'll get.

All of the above, none of the above

Some teachers have fallen in love with "all of the above" and "none of the above." You can't take one of their tests without those phrases appearing in every other question. "All of the above" is often the right answer if it is an option. And *hope* that you see it as a potential answer to *every* question because *it gives you a much better chance to do better on the test* than your mastery of the material (or lack thereof) might normally warrant. Why? Because you don't have to be really sure that "all of the above" is correct to choose it. All you have to be is *pretty* sure that *two* answers are correct (and equally sure the others are not *necessarily* wrong). As long as there is—you feel—more than one correct answer, then "all of the above" must be the right choice!

Likewise, you don't have to be convinced that "none of the above" is the right answer, just *reasonably* sure that none of the other answers are absolutely correct.

Just be careful to read those instructions! If they say, "Choose the *best* answer" and you rapidly choose "(A) the Andes," you lose if (A) is merely *a* correct answer. "(E) all of the above" will still be the *best* answer if every *other* answer is *also* correct.

A word about "easy" tests

Some people think "open book" tests are the easiest of all. They pray for them...at least until they see their first one.

These are the toughest tests of all, if only because even normally "nice" teachers feel no compunction whatsoever about making such tests as tough as a Marine drill instructor. Heck, *you can use your book!* That's like having a legal crib sheet, right? Worse yet, many open-book tests are also take-home tests, meaning you can use your notes (and any other books or tools you can think of).

Since you have to anticipate that there will be *no* easy questions, no matter how well you know the material, you need to do some preparation before you deal with this type of test:

- Mark important pages by turning down corners, using paper clips or any other method that will help you quickly flip to important charts, tables, summaries or illustrations.

- Write an index of the pages you've turned down so you know where to turn immediately for a *specific* chart, graph, table, etc.

- Summarize all important facts, formulas, etc. on a separate sheet.
- (If you are also allowed to bring your notes or it's a take-home test), write a brief index to your notes (general topics only) so you know where to find pertinent information.

Answer the questions you don't need the book for first, including those of which you're fairly sure and know where to check the answers in your book. Star these latter ones.

Then use the book. Check your starred answers first and erase the stars once you have checked. Then work on those questions on which you must rely fully on the book.

Chapter Seven

THE DAY OF THE EXAM: APPLYING WHAT YOU'VE LEARNED

"It is not enough to succeed. Others must fail."
— Gore Vidal (1925—)

"Gore Vidal grades on the curve."
— your mother

Well, here you are. No longer are you thinking of the exam as being "next month" or "next week" or even "tomorrow." You're sitting in the very room in the very chair and someone is heading your way with a test paper.

Margaret, lead the way

Right here, right at the beginning of this chapter, let me tell you about my friend Margaret. She's going to help you get there—with a technique I call the Margaret Preview.

Margaret and her husband, Bob, lived in a large capital city in a Third World country. Because of his job, they had to attend a lot of receptions and dinners at other peoples' homes, but the streets of this particular city were not very well marked and the numbering system of the houses was not all that logical.

Bob and Margaret both had a thing about punctuality, so they devised a plan. Early on the day of the party, Margaret, armed with city map and invitation, searched for the house or apartment. And she did not give up until she found it.

Due to Margaret's preparation, that night Bob and Margaret would arrive on time without having driven aimlessly around the now-dark streets searching for a house...or a whole neighborhood.

They could have been fashionably late for a party now and then. But you really don't want to be late for a test, especially something like the SAT.

If you're taking a test in a new surrounding, do the Margaret Preview. If it's in a different building or room, take a few minutes and find it. You don't want to discover 90 seconds before the bell that Room 1210A is in the West Tower and not immediately across the hall from Room 1211A in the East Tower where you are standing.

If it's off campus, check out the location a few days early. See how long it takes you (and adjust for weather, time of day and day of the week). Where is the parking? Which door do you go in? Where's the nearest place to get a cup of coffee on the morning of the exam? Is there construction? Which streets are one way? Which exit do you take from the freeway? Are there tolls?

The lifesaving bunch of stuff

Now that you're safely there, on time, what did you bring with you?

I used to make up what I called the Test Kit. Into a backpack went pens or pencils (depending on what I had to have for the test)—two or three of each; the book and workbooks associated with the test; my notes; a calculator, if allowed; a candy bar or other treat that would give me energy; photo ID, if required, and an entry card, if required.

By collecting all this mess in one place, I wouldn't be likely to forget it. Also, if I did something dreadful like oversleep, I only had to grab one thing and dash, dash, dash out the door.

You have enough to worry you the morning of a big test. Don't spend frantic minutes looking for something that you could have placed inside a backpack or briefcase or large purse the night before. Be kind to yourself.

Double your pleasure—sit alone

Unless you are already in an assigned seat, try to sit near the front so you will get the exam first and have some precious few seconds at the end while the other papers are being passed to the front. It also places you near the teacher or proctor for easier access for questions.

Avoid sitting near someone who has a lot of noisy jewelry, who is cracking or popping gum or who is too friendly with the others in the area. Be a hermit, in other words. Choose a quiet area.

Just a couple more tips: Wear loose, comfortable clothes, the kind that you love, the favorite shirt or sweater or slacks. If you're left-handed, look for a left-handed desk. Check out the room for sunlight (too much or too little), lighting and heat and cold.

The Hoosier measuring system

Remember in the movie "Hoosiers" when the team that Gene Hackman was coaching made it to the state finals? The boys walked into the fieldhouse and were overwhelmed by its size; it sure wasn't like the little gymnasiums they were used to playing in.

Gene was smart. He had them *measure the basketball court.* Whaddya know? It was exactly the same size as the one back in little Hickory. Point made. Point taken. They won, of course. (Oh, sorry, I thought you'd seen the movie.)

Pull a Gene Hackman. Take a "measure" of the exam in front of you before you begin.

Go all the way

Begin at the beginning. Then move through to the end. No, I'm not talking about taking the exam, I'm talking about looking through the booklet or taking a glance at all the questions. If you have permission to go all the way through it, do that before you even sharpen your pencil. Just give yourself an overview of what lies ahead. That way you can spot the easier sections, "star" the stumpers and get an idea of the point values assigned to each section.

The art of war

There are three ways to attack a multiple-choice test:

1. Start at the first question and keep going, question by question, until you reach the end, never leaving a question until you have either answered it fully or made an educated guess.
2. Answer every *easy* question—the ones you know the answers to without any thinking at all or those requiring the simplest calculations—first, then go back and do the harder ones.

3. Answer the *hardest* questions first, then go back and do the easy ones.

None of these three options is inherently right or wrong. Each may work for different individuals. (And I'm assuming that these three approaches are all in the context of the test format. Weighted sections may well affect your strategy.)

The first approach is, in one sense, the quickest, in that no time is wasted reading through the whole test trying to pick out either the easiest or hardest questions. Presuming that you do not allow yourself to get stumped by a single question so that you spend an inordinate amount of time on it, it is probably the method most of you employ.

Remember, though, to leave questions that confuse you from the outset to the end and allocate enough time to both go back to those you haven't answered and check *all* your answers thoroughly.

The second approach ensures that you will maximize your right answers—you're putting those you are certain of down first.

It may also, presuming that you knock off these easy ones relatively fast, give you the most time to work on those that you find particularly vexing.

Many experts recommend this method because they maintain that answering so many questions one after another gives you immediate confidence to tackle the questions you're not sure about. If you find that you agree, then by all means use this strategy. However, you may consider just *noting* the easy ones as you preread the test. This takes less time and, to me, delivers the same "confidence boost."

The last approach is actually the one I use.

In fact, I make it a point to do the very hardest question first, then work my way "down" the difficulty ladder.

It may sound like a strange strategy to you, so let me explain the psychology.

First of all, I figure if time pressure starts getting to me at the end of the test, I would rather be in a position to answer the easiest questions—and a lot of them—in the limited time left than ones I really have to think about. After all, by the end of the test, my mind won't be working as well as at the beginning!

And that's a major benefit of the third approach: When I am most "up," most awake, most alert, I am tackling those questions that require the most analysis, thinking, interpretation, etc. When I am most tired—near the end—I am answering the questions that are virtually "gimmes."

At the same time, I am also giving myself a *real* shot of confidence. As soon as I finish the first hard question, I already feel better. When I finish all of the hard ones, everything is downhill.

It is not the approach for everybody, but it may be for you.

I would always, however, try to ensure adequate time to at least put down an answer for every question. Better to get one question wrong and complete three other answers than get one right and leave three blank.

And don't fall into the "answer daze," that blank stare some students get when they can't think of an answer—for 10 minutes.

Do *some*thing.

Better to move on and get that one question wrong than waste invaluable time doing nothing.

Ask questions immediately if you don't understand something. The proctor may not be able to say anything (or may not know anything to say), but it's worth a try.

If you get part of a question answered and you need to return to finish it but you can't figure it out, work out a little code for yourself. Put a symbol in the margin beside the problem that translates as "I'm partly done here—come back to this one after I've done all the ones I can do."

Guess and guess again?

If you do guess at any of the objective questions and you are getting your test paper returned to you, place a little dot or other symbol beside them. That way you will know how successful your guessing was. For example, suppose you guessed at 30 questions and you got 22 of them right. That tells me your guesses are, for the most part, *educated* guesses, not wild stabs in the dark, and that you earned enough points to make it worthwhile, *even if you got penalized for missing eight others.* However, if you only got six right, review my comments on educated guessing. Something's not working right for you.

When you think you have finished with a section, double-check to see if that's true. Look on the answer sheet or in the blue book to make sure all the questions have been answered.

It's time to figure this one out

Pace yourself. If you have 40 multiple-choice questions and you have 20 minutes allotted for that section, you don't have to be MIT material to figure that you should spend a maximum of 30 seconds on each answer. Check your progress two or three times during the 20 minutes.

Which reminds me: Don't depend on a wall clock. Bring your watch. Some students like to remove it and place it on the desk so they can see it without having to look at their wrist, especially if the writing hand and the watch hand are different.

You say oral and I say aural

Listen up.

When the teacher (or tape recorder) gives you a question, jot down the key words so that you can refer to them when you think up your answer.

Do the same thing if you are being given a dictation where you are expected to listen, then write down what you heard. Key words—the nouns and verbs—will help you "capture" the rest of the sentence.

If you don't understand the question (whether it's in a foreign language you're studying or in English), ask to have it repeated. Ask again if you still don't understand. Listen intently to everything.

For computer-scored tests

If you are required to fill in a little rectangle to show which answer is correct so that a machine can score the results, mark the answer sheet very carefully. Stray pencil marks can be picked up by the computer, causing the wrong answer to be recorded. If you carefully filled in one box, only to change your mind later, completely, *completely* erase the first answer. If the computer picks up both markings, guess what happens? You don't get a point, even if one of the boxes is correct.

No post-break dancing, please

Take the breaks that are offered. You'll benefit in the long run by going to the bathroom, getting a drink of water, eating a candy bar, or all of the above, rather than sitting there working through another algebraic equation, if you're allowed to go on working.

Just as you needed the good sleep you got during the week, you'll need to be energized by the breaks. Besides, suppose you didn't move, and then, 20 minutes after the break, you've got to go the bathroom. Desperately. What if the proctor won't let you? Do you kill him and take the ACT while in prison at West Bubba, Arkansas? Or do you act smart and take the break when everyone else does?

They'll never kick sand in your face again

You can perform some unobtrusive exercises at your desk that will make you feel refreshed. Try them right now. First, tense up your feet—squeeze them hard, then relax them, then squeeze them. Do the same with the muscles in your calves, shoulders, hips and abdomen. It's a pretty simple exercise but I find it energizes me when I am unable to get up and move around the room. Even moving the facial muscles helps. Do them looking down at your paper, or otherwise your teacher will think you are making faces at her or that you are having a coronary.

If there is time, review. Go back and check over answers to essay questions that may not be as complete as you'd like them to be, or look again at the unanswered questions in any other section.

If you have even more time, look at the "guess" questions you've marked. Does anything suddenly make sense, making you change your mind? Remember what I said about going with your first choice, but if you suddenly remember that the Catskills are in New York and not in North Dakota, change the answer!

For my next trick

If you've just finished a big, big test, get out of town. Go to a movie or a party or something that will allow you to forget, for a few hours, that you have been keeping your nose to the grindstone for the past several days.

Go. Relax. Then go on to Chapter 8.

Chapter Eight

POST-TEST:
SURVIVAL AND REVIEW

"Winning isn't everything, but wanting to win is."
—Vince Lombardi (1913-1970)

"Winning is everything."
—your mother

No, it's not, Mom. But you and I know what she's talking about, don't we? It's nice to win, whether it's a noontime intramural basketball game or getting an "A" on an exam.

And, don't you agree, it feels even better to "win" when the exam has been tough, when it's been challenging and difficult, than when it was one of Mr. Bibble's easy unit tests.

Vince got it right. Wanting to win is important. Otherwise, why did you study so hard and give up so much for so long?

"Ace" Any Test

Now that you've done the studying and taken the test, you want to know the results.

Let's assume you did well. Congratulations! But, no matter how many points you earned, reviewing the test is a vitally important exercise in preparing yourself for the next test—and for taking a hard look at the entire way you study.

If you take a standardized test and you are offered the chance to get a copy of the exam—and your own answers—do so. It may cost you a few bucks, but I definitely think it's worth it.

It's unlikely you'll find they made any mistakes in the scoring of the exam, but it will be good exercise for you to review what you got right and what you didn't while the test is reasonably fresh in your mind.

The emphasis in this chapter, however, is on the tests you take from teachers. Most will review the overall results of the test with the class on the day they are returned. First of all, you want to make sure the answers that you missed are truly incorrect. Teachers make mistakes. I know that's going to come as a shock.

Don't make a nuisance of yourself by challenging everything in class, waving your hand and saying, in a pleading voice, "But, but, Mr. Squeezicks! I meant to say George Washington Carver instead of George Washington"!

Concentrate on the answers that are clearly marked wrong. Even a semi-alert student evaluating his or her own exam can grab a couple of extra points and those points can move you up another letter grade.

If the question really was ambiguous and your answer could arguably be as correct as the one the teacher chose, go ahead and make a pitch. This will be especially effective if a few others in the class chose the same answer. (There is strength in numbers.)

Your chances will be a lot better if you keep the discussion on a diplomatic level, of course, rather than getting snotty or snide. Teachers can get so defensive sometimes!

Now, let's suppose you did get the answer wrong, fair and square. Most likely, you got it wrong for one of the following reasons:

You made a careless mistake

1. You wrote down the wrong letter or number. You knew the answer was (A), but, in your haste, you wrote down (B).
2. Similarly, you filled in the wrong box in the answer sheet. You see the mistake now. You vow not to do it again. (Good. That's the first step on the road to recovery.)
3. You left out a whole section of the test because you didn't turn the page, or you "thought" you had done it or...
4. You wrote in such a scribbled fashion or crammed the words together so much that the teacher pulled an "I can't read it so it's wrong" deal on you and gave you no credit. (I'm on his side. Get your act—and your penmanship—together.)
5. You misread the directions. You missed the slightly important word "not," so you provided the exact opposite of what you should have.
6. You guessed wildly without even reading the options and ignored the fact that points would be deducted for wrong answers, so you got fewer points than if you had left the answer sheet blank for those questions.

You didn't know the material

1. You didn't read all the assignments, or get a complete set of class notes, or find out answers to questions you had about some of the information.
2. You attended class, took notes and read the assignments, but you didn't understand what the topic was all about.
3. You needed to know a lot of facts—dates, names, events, causes and effects—and you didn't.

Your personal life loomed too large

1. You brought into the test your worries that the person you're dating is going to dump you, that your parents are fighting again, that your kids are heading to reform school if you don't do something right now or...whatever.
2. You had a horrible cold, a terrible headache or you got too little or too much sleep.

Next time I'll know better

Don't beat up on yourself too much. Do take time to evaluate how you did—the bad and the good. Go for the positive. Maybe you always hated essay questions and this time you did well. It's as important to evaluate why you *were* successful as why you *weren't*.

In that case, maybe you learned from your study group. Maybe your teacher gave you some good advice. Maybe you read that section of this book first and it helped you (I like that choice). Maybe you're picking up reading and comprehension skills from a combination of factors. Do think back over what you may have done differently this time. Give yourself a lot of the credit. After all, you took the test all by yourself. Pat-on-the-back time! The worrisome part is the "careless mistake" area, yet it's probably the easiest to deal with. Take a vow that you won't do such silly things again. It's especially annoying when you had the right answer and you simply circled the wrong one. Next time? Pay a little closer attention to what you're doing and pace yourself so you can double-check your work.

There's no substitute for knowledge

If you go into the test knowing only half the material, don't expect to get above the 50-percent mark. Doing well on a test, as I've been telling you all along, is a combination of knowing how to take the test and knowing the stuff that goes into the answers.

If you can't seem to get prepared, maybe you'd better go back and reread those earlier chapters. Get to class, get your work organized, manage your time, read the book, do your homework, the whole *shtick.*

Now's the time to see where the teacher got the questions that made up the test. What percentage of the test came from the lectures? From the book? From the handouts?

It is unlikely that you're going to get an "A" in every class you take, but you can get the best grade possible. Even in classes that, for whatever reason, are way, way over your head, you can at least pass. And, in most cases, you're going to do a lot better than that.

Ask questions. Ask questions during class. Ask questions when you meet with your teacher. Join a study group and ask questions. Ask questions when the test results are being discussed.

Pity parties are "out" this year

What nerve you have! A personal life, you say? But isn't Chemistry 104 or American Government more important?

Of course not. But turn the personal motor off now and then and spend time with your friends down at the Continental Congress.

Yes, we all have colds and sore feet and heartbreaks. That is life, after all. But we can compartmentalize the parts of our life now and then without going overboard with it. Remember the Imelda Marcos Theory.

Guess how you did

Don't forget to see how many of your "guesses" you got right. Naturally, the better you know the material, the fewer guesses you need to make, but on some big tests you may have a lot of them.

And the door prize goes to...

After you've sacrificed to get a good grade on the exam, treat yourself. A little fun-and-games reward system is in order. You study really hard for four hours, have a candy bar. You get a B on the quiz over the French Revolution, go to a movie.

When you have something to look forward to, even though you realize it's a game (hey, life is a game, so play along!), it makes it "fun" to push yourself in order to kick back and relax.

Let's try that one again, shall we?

If you really messed up on the test, sit down with your teacher and discuss the reasons (having first done your self-evaluation, based on the areas mentioned in this chapter).

Ask if you can take another test—you may not be able to get any credit for it, but you'll impress him and he will look more kindly upon you when it comes time to enter your final grade on the official form.

Retaking "bad" tests is a good idea for another reason. Unless you just completely messed up in getting the right answers matched to the right questions, you probably did so poorly because you didn't know the material well enough the first time.

Now you are giving yourself a second chance to learn material that will no doubt appear on more tests in future, and—now this may come as a real shock—you might actually need to know this information for some reason in your future life.

And, a satisfactory completion of the retake will give you a boost of self-confidence that got stomped on when you got a bad grade the first time. Hey, you're saying to the Test Demons, I can do this!

Come with me now to the inner sanctum

I've been talking to you about what you can and should do. Now, let's take a peek in the next chapter at this whole test business from the teacher's point of view. C'mon, he won't bite.

Chapter Nine

HOW TEACHERS MAKE UP TESTS

"Examinations are formidable even to the best prepared, for the greatest fool may ask more than the wisest man can answer."
—Charles Caleb Colton (1780?-1832)

Apparently, Mr. Colton had just flunked his mid-term.

You've got one advantage over Colton: You're going to read this chapter and learn how the "greatest fools" make up those tests.

I have to admit that some teachers, I am sorry to report, look upon tests as ways to beat down challenges to their authority ("I'll show them who knows this stuff!") or as punishment ("That'll teach them not to love English lit!"), but fortunately the key word here is "some."

Let's ignore the paranoid and sadistic and look at how a *typical* teacher makes up a test.

I'm just an average kind of guy

If students who have studied and made a valid attempt to do well on the test earn a test grade that ranges from "excellent" to "good" to "average" (i.e., A to B to C), then this tells them where they stand. It also tells the *teacher* where he or she stands.

If the test results show everyone getting an A or everyone getting Ds and Fs (after honest attempts to do well), the teacher has messed up.

On correctly prepared and fairly scored tests, the majority of students will get Bs and Cs, with a small number getting As and Ds. There should be an even smaller number of Fs, "rewards" for those who truly don't have a clue or who don't care.

The test is, after all, a test of the teacher, too. The teacher has an obligation to give you information, help you understand that information, make assignments that have some validity, and take you progressively through a series of learning exercises.

The test should reflect your understanding of this body of knowledge. The burden is on you to do the work and learn the material; there is an additional burden on the teacher to make sure everyone (except those who don't care) is actually learning.

The wise teacher provides several opportunities during the semester to "test" how well you are learning. Quizzes (scheduled and surprise ones), papers, reports, projects, tests on units, chapters or whole books, oral reports, etc. All of this should add up to your evaluation—your grade.

Some teachers love one type of question. Some are True-False Freaks; others push the Multiple-Choice/Short Answer

Combo. If old tests, old students, the teacher's own comments on the test coming up and your own experience tell you this is true, you might as well study for that kind of test. You still have to know the material, of course. It's just that you may need to remind yourself that you're going to have to deal with it in a particular fashion.

The best teachers use a combination of test questions to find out what you know. Frankly, some of them hate grading essay questions so they rarely use them.

Why do teachers choose essay questions?

1. They are easier and less time-consuming to prepare.
2. They may be preferred when a group is small and the test will not be reused.
3. They are used to explore student's attitudes rather than measure his or her achievements.
4. They are used to encourage and reward the development of student skill in writing.
5. They are suitable when it's important for the students to explain or describe.
6. They are more suitable to some material. You're likely to have more essay questions in English and history than you are in the sciences.

Teachers use objective questions because:

1. They are preferred when the group is large and the test may be reused.
2. They are more efficient when highly reliable test scores must be obtained quickly.
3. They are more suitable for covering a larger amount of content in the same amount of time.

4. They are easier for the teacher to give an impartial grade. Whether it's the good student or the bad, the good essay writer or the lousy one, everyone has to write down (C) to get number 22 correct.
5. They are easier for some teachers to create.
6. They may be used when students need to demonstrate or show.

A thousand points of right

At the time that the teacher decides what kinds of questions he will ask and determines what each question will cover, he must also assign a point value to each question.

He is going to assign higher point values to questions that are concerned with material that has been emphasized by his lectures and class discussions and by the reading. He will also assign more points to areas of the test that will require more time and attention.

Think about it: You've never taken a test where each true-false question was worth 20 points and the long essay was worth five. He will clearly show the points possible for each section and/or question so you can decide how to spend your time.

Teachers have check lists, too

The teacher has selected the material to be covered. He's told you, at least in general terms, what the test will cover. He has decided on the format of the test, assigned points and written the questions, then done his own double-checking to make sure he has included everything he wanted to include.

He has also made sure that the questions this semester are different from the ones on previous tests as he suspects that some of you little devils will be looking at them, hoping against hope that he will provide the same questions again.

He has set up the test in a readable format so there is no confusion, and has made sure it is free of typos. He has checked his questions and answers to make sure they are not ambiguous.

Should we give him a passing grade?

The "test" for him comes when he sits down to grade what you've done. If half the students completely messed up one of the questions—but messed it up in the same way—he has to admit that the directions were not clearly written. He may even decide to throw out the question.

He has determined that the number and complexity of the questions are suitable for the time allotted for the test. If he consistently finds that even his best students only completed half the test, he had too much on the test. And, hopefully, will shorten future ones.

A key word that the teacher has to remind himself to use in making up and in grading a test is "reasonable." What is a *reasonable* number of questions students can be expected to answer in 45 minutes? What should a teacher *reasonably* expect students to know from these chapters?

You can learn to fake sincerity

No, you can't. I just said that to keep your attention. In this chapter on teachers, let me leave you with this thought about your relationship with those who instruct you:

Teachers do like students (and give them better grades) if they show a genuine interest in the subject matter and in the class. You don't have to be a Teacher's Pet or Nerd of the Month. But feel free to show that you like what you're learning.

And if you've decided that chemistry is far down on your dislike list along with public speaking and serious leg cramps, don't vent your anger, hatred and snide remarks to your teacher. Look. He loves this stuff. He even goes to conventions where there are other chemistry teachers. He spends his weekends reading books like *50 Ways to Make Milkshakes with Hydrochloric Acid.* Just endure. Do the best you can. Smile. And—best of all—go to him with honest questions about material that you can't or don't understand. He's there to help you.

Fill in the blank so you won't go blank

I'll leave you with one more thing—the item I referred to back in Chapter 4. On the next page is the form that I've designed to help you sort out what you've got to do when, where and how.

Stop! Don't fill this out. Photocopy it, then fill in the blanks.

There. I've said it. I'm done. And you're just getting started.

Remember this: Don't ever say again, "She gave me a C!" No, *she* didn't. Your teachers don't give you grades. You give yourself the grades you deserve, the grades you earned by either studying or goofing off.

So, what grade are you going to give yourself this next time?

"Ace" Any Test

PRE-TEST ORGANIZER

CLASS:_____ TEACHER: _____
TEST DATE:_____TIME: From _____to _____
PLACE:_____

SPECIAL INSTRUCTIONS to myself (e.g., take calculator, dictionary, etc.):_____
_____

MATERIALS I NEED to study for this test (check all needed):

     ❑ Book   ❑ Tapes/Videos
     ❑ Workbook   ❑ Old Tests
     ❑ Class Notes   ❑ Other
     ❑ Handouts   ❑ _____

THE FORMAT of the test will be (write the number of T/F, essays, mult.-choice, etc., and total points for each section):
_____
_____
_____
_____
_____

STUDY GROUP MEETINGS (times, places):
1._____
2._____
3._____
4._____
5._____

MATERIAL TO BE COVERED:

Indicate topics, sources and amount of review (light or heavy) required. Check box when review is completed.

Topic	Sources	Review
_____	_____	❑ ____
_____	_____	❑ ____
_____	_____	❑ ____
_____	_____	❑ ____
_____	_____	❑ ____
_____	_____	❑ ____
_____	_____	❑ ____
_____	_____	❑ ____
_____	_____	❑ ____

AFTER THE TEST:

Grade I expected _____ Grade I received _____

What did I do that helped me? _____

_____

_____

_____

_____

_____

What else should I have done?

_____

_____

_____

_____

_____

_____

"Ace" Any Test

INDEX